The giG It's a Girl Thing
Volume 1

Take a journey of self-discovery where
no masks are required.

Embrace your own kind of **fabulous**!

Celeste-Kuri

WESTBOW
PRESS
A DIVISION OF THOMAS NELSON

WestBow Press books may be ordered through booksellers or by contacting:

WestBow Press
A Division of Thomas Nelson
1663 Liberty Drive
Bloomington, IN 47403
www.westbowpress.com
1-(866) 928-1240

Because of the dynamic nature of the Internet, any web addresses or links contained in this book may have changed since publication and may no longer be valid. The views expressed in this work are solely those of the author and do not necessarily reflect the views of the publisher, and the publisher hereby disclaims any responsibility for them.

ISBN: 978-1-4497-9790-4 (sc)
ISBN: 978-1-4497-9791-1 (hc)
ISBN: 978-1-4497-9789-8 (e)

Library of Congress Control Number: 2013910612

Any people depicted in stock imagery provided by Shutterstock are models, and such images are being used for illustrative purposes only. Certain stock imagery © Shutterstock.

Printed in the United States of America.

WestBow Press rev. date: 12/27/2013

Scripture quotations marked NIV are taken from the HOLY BIBLE, NEW INTERNATIONAL VERSION®, Copyright © 1973, 1978, 1984 International Bible Society. Used by permission of Zondervan. All rights reserved.

Scripture quotations marked MSG are taken from The Message. Copyright © 1993, 1994, 1995, 1996, 2000, 2001, 2002. Used by permission of NavPress Publishing Group.

Scripture quotations marked NCV taken from the New Century Version®. Copyright © 2005 by Thomas Nelson, Inc. Used by permission. All rights reserved.

Scripture quotations marked CEB taken from the Common English Bible®.

Scripture quotations marked AMP are taken from the Amplified® Bible, Copyright © 1954, 1958, 1962, 1964, 1965, 1987 by The Lockman Foundation. Used by permission.

Scripture quotations marked NLT are taken from the Holy Bible, New Living Translation, copyright 1996, 2004. Used by permission of Tyndale House Publishers., Wheaton, Illinois 60189. All rights reserved.

Stories written are inspired by true stories. Some of the names have been changed for the privacy each individual.

Disclaimer: Some of the anecdotal stories in this book are true and are included with the permission of the persons involved. All other stories are composites of real situations, and any resemblance to people, living or dead, is coincidental.

For You

I dedicate this book to every girlfriend who is searching for a deep connection and personal relationship with our Creator and to the girlfriends who are seriously passionate, bold, and courageous about leaving an imprint in our world!

A passionate giG!

XOXO

Contents

Preface

This guide, together with the giG, volume 2, *Finding the Best things in Life: True Friendship, Great Coffee, and Fabulous Shoes*, can be used as tools to help girlfriends form alliances with women all over our world who are not afraid of running the race and pursuing what we have all been called to do! No matter where you are in your spiritual walk—whether you are new to Christianity, a mature leader of women's ministry, or are in any other phase of your life—it doesn't matter! It's about coming together and exhorting one another, not to be hearers but doers of His Word, taking His message of love, grace, and salvation everywhere we go. It is to serve those in need and each other by doing acts of kindness and at times leading dangerous commissions that require boldness and courage!

When we join this link of girlfriends in God, we are sure to witness miracles, see lives transformed, and hopefully bring a little piece of heaven here to earth. Become a girlfriend in God, commit to lead a group, and help inspire others to do what we have been called to do!

Serving is not just a privilege; it's a responsibility! Join the rest of the giG, and become a part of a platform that will change you and a piece of our world!

Gracias

I am grateful for the amazing people God has put in my life to teach, guide, encourage, and inspire me. I've met many remarkable people from different backgrounds and walks of life who have touched my life and left an impression that will last a lifetime. It's been a privilege to know these individuals, whose courage to live and smile, regardless of their adversity, gives me hope. It also fuels my drive to never stop doing what we have all been called to do.

My brother Oscar is my biggest inspiration. The way he sees the beauty in life and loves unconditionally is something all of us should learn to emulate. He is the epitome of kindness and the closest you will get to meeting an angel here on earth.

Jose Carlos's courage to face the world without holding back is beyond admirable; we need more people like him in our world. He is amazing!

Thanks to Martalicia for being a faithful servant of God. Even while enduring physical pain; nothing stops her from taking God's Word everywhere she goes. I learned from her the true meaning of perseverance; she is a remarkable example to follow.

To Sonia, my mentor, because of her unconditional love for teaching me about the Word of God, made an enormous impact in my life that will last forever.

I'm grateful for Veronica. She taught me such practical ways of solving issues and for always believing in me. Her words of encouragement, leadership, and incredible teaching gave me strength.

Thanks to Holly, a woman whose tenacity, passion, and zest for life gave me the courage to become unstoppable in the discovery of God's purpose for my life.

To my brilliant husband, whose wisdom kept me from flying over the cuckoo's nest; and to my amazing daughters, Nicollette and Victoria. Nicollette, I want to be like you when I grow up. I am also so grateful for Victoria's never-ending desire to make sure I am always okay. I thank them for being patient and withstanding the countless hours of writing as I missed out on watching movies while they ate *papitas con limon*.

To my mother and my sister, without whom I have no clue where I'd be! Words can't describe the gratitude I have for *all* they have done for me. To Carmen, who knows me so well that even if I don't say a word, she knows what I need. And of course thanks to the first generation of the giG: Denise, Michelle, Liza, Lily, and Kelley.

To all single moms and to the wives and mothers who take care of their husbands or children with a special need, disability, and especially my sister in-law Betty. You have my utmost respect. Because of your constant loving ways, you demonstrate commitment, devotion, and undying love. I am moved beyond words. I admire you, and please know your ways teach me.

To every soldier, and soldier's wife, individual and families I've had the honor of knowing and serving through Send Me

Foundation. I am thankful to be able to bring a smile when you are facing hardship.

I am forever grateful for having been a part of your life, even if it was only for a short moment with some of you. I am a better person because of all of you. Thank you for dancing and singing in my life! May the windows of heaven open wide and an overflow of blessings pour over your lives!

Thank you! I love you!

Off we go on an incredible adventure! It may get bumpy,

but the outcome will be amazing!

Are you ready to begin a change

in the generations to come?

Let's do this!

Let's giG it!

I pray that something within you will ignite as you read this. Whether it's for the first time or it's been dormant for a while, it's time to awaken and discover Jesus' purpose for your life.

I pray we commit to take God's message to the world—and make some noise while we do it! I pray we demonstrate that we are strong and capable women. I pray we bring a bigger piece of heaven on earth to everyone around us but especially to those who are in need and have lost hope. I pray we leave an imprint, dancing and singing everywhere we go! I pray we come to be instruments of hope and give the greatest gift of love—Jesus

Make your life count!

Celeste-Kuri

Introduction

A Journey of Self-Discovery

Wow, life is beautiful! I began this journey back in 1995, when I was only one signature away from becoming a divorcee. I thank God for second chances. The journey here was not made up of all happy days. I am an ordinary woman like you, with issues, goals, and dreams. I want to share my story although there was much heartache and pain, and I almost gave up, the story took a turn. And now I hope to encourage others who find themselves in similar situations. Anyone can start something, but it takes courage to finish anything. My journey took a lot of determination and boldness. My husband and I went through a lot, and when I say a lot, I mean muchisimo! And through it all, hope was restored, and deep faith was ignited. I am confident my story can bring hope to someone who's lost it, because if it happened to me, it can happen to you! I want to share more about a few things I am very passionate about, and it begins with understanding God's love!

When my husband and I were having difficulties, we were invited to partake in a couples group. At the time I was so done with trying to make my marriage work. I felt like I had tried everything. I had spoken to so many psychologists, therapists, and even priests. We had countless arguments about his eager desire for us to reconcile. He often said to me that I was the love of his life and he could never imagine his life without me. I heard this, but my immaturity didn't allow me to actually listen.

I come from a traditional Hispanic background, and the truth is, church for me meant attending first communions, baptisms, weddings, and of course occasional Sundays here and there. Later I realized that knowing about God and actually knowing God are very different things. I often have conversations with people, and so many of their answers regarding religion are given by instinct. I get it; I have been there. When I ask, "Why do you have to do certain things?" or "What does this mean?" and especially, "What do we have to do to go to heaven?" Many answer something like this, "Because it's what we are supposed to do" This is another common reply when people don't know the reason; "I am not really sure"

There is a big difference between religion and having a personal relationship with God. I guess you could say I sort of thought I knew about my religion, but I didn't really have a relationship with God—not a personal or intimate one anyway. I like to use this as an example: Can you say you know Oprah? We know quite a lot of facts about her, where she comes from, the journey that got her to where she is, etc., and because we've seen her on TV so much, we feel like we do know her. We know she's done amazing things, so we figure she must be a good person. But do we really know her? Get my point?

I remember having a few conversations with God that sounded a little something like this: *I know You're supposed to be perfect and all, but I think You made a tiny mistake in thinking Fernando (my husband) and I are supposed to stay together forever.* Fernando and I had years of never-ending disagreements, and that's putting it mildly. Our arguments were quite dreadful; I would name our fights like natural disasters. Some were like tsunamis (la Niña) others felt like earthquakes (la Pinta), and a few like hurricanes, (la Santa Maria) and at times they were like all three together; la Niña, la Pinta, y la Santa Maria!! Ay,ay,ay!

I am very outspoken, and a bit more impulsive. Okay way more! And he on the other hand, is an observer and when it comes to serious matters, he waits to answer until he's sure; this way he avoids making foolish mistakes. (I know what some of you are thinking, that I should take a hint ☺) He's responsible, hardworking, and extremely devoted to our family, and he never, ever saw divorce as an option. I, on the other hand, used the D-word as a regular part of my vocabulary.

Fernando is a remarkably committed man who more than anything is determined to keep his family together forever. I am sure you are probably wondering, what was I thinking? Why would I consider leaving a man with such qualities? Hold on, remember there is always more to every story, besides it takes one to argue (that would be me) but two to fight. (That would be both of us)

At the beginning of my journey to restoring our marriage, it was uncomfortable for me to modify certain things. It wasn't easy for me to admit my wrongs, and hearing the word *submission* gave me chills and made my stomach queasy. However, it all makes perfect sense now. To submit does not mean to bow down; it's different.

A good example is the fact that we must submit to authority, whether it's a teacher, a boss, or a police officer. More often than we are willing to admit, we dislike the feeling of having to yield to someone; our human nature frequently believes we are right. And on many occasions, having to answer, "Yes sir," alerts us of how egotism and smugness get in the way and we feel like rebelling. But we know there are laws we must follow to have order. If we abide by them, it works for the best.

I was so angry when Fernando agreed to attend the couples group, where the leaders were Christians and we weren't. It felt as if I was going into a cult. What convinced me to stay was the fact that the friends who invited us were normal in every way. They have a wonderful marriage, and their family is so lovely. Another reason that helped me decide to take a chance on the group was the fact that the rest of the people attending also had issues and broken marriages, and they were desperately hoping this cult or whatever it was would help them.

I decided I was not going to argue every point, want immediate answers to every question, and especially demand all the attention, like I did almost always! (Wow, I was horrible!) I finally put my guard down. We received help to rescue what was left of our dying marriage, and that was when everything changed. I followed instructions and vowed not to make any convenient changes. I decided to do this God and Bible thing step by step, like a recipe to the best diet or detox ever. Essentially I had to acquire the ingredients necessary and not substitute any of them. It was the first real commitment I had ever made.

After all the years my husband and I have been together, we never cease to hear the question from those who know about our story, "How were you able to reconcile and love him the way you do?" The answer is simple depending on what you truly hope for your relationship, yet to some it can be very complex.

You are the only one who can answer that. What you desire for your marriage is a personal choice. If you want to check a box in your "I tried everything to fix this" list, then you will do just that. You will check the box and hope you won't have to deal with guilt when it comes to facing your children. You will probably go through the motions without any real emotions because unless you surrender to God, you will not be able to do this—not on your own.

Believe me when I say that knowing about God and really knowing Him are the keys to real success. I may not know much about other matters, but I do know He is the answer. There are thousands of women like me who say they've tried everything but fail to see they need to go to the Creator of marriage to get long-lasting solutions. They don't understand that marriage has a certain order we must learn about and follow. Egos and pride have no room in this covenant.

Remember when you first met your husband? If you haven't met him yet, know this: You will want to spend every moment with him as you slowly but surely realize you are falling in love. Your heart will yearn to know everything there is to know about him, and you will do whatever you can to spend as much time with him as possible. You will realize that every time you are together makes you feel safe and happy, and that brings an overwhelming sense of peace. That's how it should feel when you begin a real, honest, and intimate relationship with Jesus. You will have a never-ending thirst for Him. When you follow through and begin to spend time with Him, it produces true intimacy, and a personal relationship develops.

There are marriages that are definitely better off apart, but before we give up, we must do everything in God's power to give it a real chance to make it. If you are single, divorced, or divorced but in a relationship, understanding and applying this to your new relationship will raise your probability of having a successful marriage by a lot!

For those of you, who are struggling to find solutions in your relationships, ask yourself this question: *Have I truly surrendered to God, to do His will and not mine?*

If you are serious about reconciling and falling in love with your spouse all over again, my advice is to choose God. Commit to follow Him in everything you do and in everything you are. There must be no substituting, no modifying for your convenience, no changing the rules; just follow what the Word says and you will begin to see things with different eyes. It's like borrowing glasses from God and getting a clearer view of how He sees us.

I have so much to learn about many things in life, and I can't wait, since I enjoy being a full-time student of life. But one thing I can say with the utmost respect and authority is that your life can be transformed if you let Him. I decided to let go and let God. And it's as if I was literally born again in every way. Now I understand that term *born-again*. Things that used to make sense to me don't anymore and things that didn't make sense do now.

Once you give your life to Jesus and make Him the pilot and not the co-pilot of your life, you comprehend life much better. Your insecurities, and erroneous ways of thinking or acting, and especially your selfish ways, are transformed. What used to be, "I need this or that to be happy," develops into, "What can I do to make you happy?" You find that the world does not revolve around you. Inconformity changes to a grateful heart, anger and shame turn into grace and forgiveness, and what you once saw as an utter mess becomes a work in progress.

If you own a Ford vehicle, why would you take it to get fixed at a BMW dealership? They will probably be aware of some of the issues the car has and may even do a quick fix; but some things only Ford can take care of, since Ford designed it. Capish? It's the same principle with relationships. It's great to get advice from a couple whose marriage is in great shape, and if your parents are a good example to follow, by all means take the good and hopefully discard the not so good. However, to have a long-lasting marriage, you must go to God.

Once I truly gave my life to Jesus, and decided to follow Him, life had meaning. I realized I had gotten a second chance, and I must not waste it. There was a reason why I had gone through everything I'd gone through in my life, the good, the bad, and the ugly. As a society it's easy for us to have shadowy outlines of what is thought to be right. Often when we follow our parents' example and if we don't learn a better way, we end up doing the things we disliked so much when we were growing up and swore we would never do. But our parents didn't always know the best way. Some of it is good, and some is not. We can't blame them; they did what they could with what they knew. Most likely they too were following their parent's pattern.

God can take an ugly situation and turn it into something beautiful if you allow Him to work in you and through you. The first big lesson I ever learned is that God's love transforms and never fails!

My life has not been all easy. The mistakes I've made left scars that took a long time to heal. But I am completely convinced it was supposed to happen in the way it did. I am able to speak with authority in regard to letting go and letting God in your life. No matter where you've been or what you've done, God loves you and accepts you as-is! I have witnessed firsthand the miracle of reconciliation.

If I had not gone through *la Niña, la Pinta, and la Santa Maria*, I would not be here today.

I recently re-married a new man—a new and improved version, that is. Fernando is definitely not the same man he was when I first met him. The old version is gone! Fernando is the perfect man for me; I can't tell you how foolish I feel for the silly conversations I had with God way back in the day, thinking God had made a mistake. After twenty-five years, I am more in love with Fernando today than I ever was. This journey has taken both of us through a narrow path, and with commitment and courage, we traveled through it and made it! Moreover, it helped seal our marriage with God's Holy Spirit. I am dedicated to our lives together forever.

Now that we have two daughters, my husband and I are devoted to inspire them to know Jesus intimately and encourage them to seek Him first. Last but not least, we desire to teach them of God's love for them and the amazing miracles they will have the privilege of witnessing as they walk with Him today, tomorrow, and forever. My mentor always taught me that for our children we pray on our knees, so I do. I pray that they will be commended with husbands who love God and in turn will understand commitment and true love.

"Delight in Him, and he will give you the desires of your heart!" (Ps. 37:4 CEB). "Enjoy serving the Lord, and he will give you whatever you ask for" (Ps. 37:4 ERV). I continuously tell my daughters this because with certainty I know God keeps His promises!

Q: Have you fully understood the depth of God's undying love for you? Do you completely understand that His love transforms? Have you taken your broken relationship to the Creator of relationships? Have you tried His way and put your way aside? What do you want to teach your children about relationships? Have you learned what is truly important in life? What?

Q: Do you now know the battles that are worth fighting for? Are you afraid to make a real commitment to God? If so, why?

Last Thoughts

So you see this is my story and the journey that got me to where I am today. It's the traveled path of how and why I got to this precise moment in time. Everything I write in this book about my family and my friends; are stories that taught me big lessons. Spanish is my first language; and I am not an English Major. I say this because no doubt you will probably find mistakes along the way. I apologize in advance, but please keep in mind it's about the message I hope to convey; not my ability to write.

These are my experiences, my perspective, but God's truth. And though life is not always easy, I learned to take things slower; and walk firmly one day at a time knowing God is with me every step of the way.

I challenge you to take a moment to evaluate your life. Ask yourself if your way of doing *"life"* has worked for you thus far? Are you happy? Are you living but not really enjoying life? Have you any room left to enhance your existence? If you haven't given this God-thing a real and honest chance, and I mean without making any convenient changes or modifications to suit your needs or lifestyle, I dare you to begin today! God's love is powerful! And that's why I believe life is beautiful!

- What left an imprint?

Listen to the music that makes

Your heart skip a beat.

Dance like no one is watching.

One day we will

Dance together in heaven!

Chapter 1

What's It Gonna Take?

I was nine years old when my brother was diagnosed with a brain tumor. Needless to say, our family's dynamics were altered forever.

After my brother's prognosis, his chances of living past the coma stage were very slim. It's been a bumpy road, but he has remained faithful to God through it all. It's been like a twenty-first-century version of Job. Oscar has endured one thing after another, but his faith has remained as solid as an oak. He wasn't supposed to have children, according to the doctors. Oscar is not only married to an incredible woman who we know was specifically handpicked for him, but he is also the father of two beautiful daughters and one awesome son. He also recently became the grandfather of two lovely little girls.

My brother became a lighted torch for me. I've often encountered difficulty in trying to launch my venture of helping others in need, and it has been challenging at times. There have been moments when I've wanted to give up, but

Oscar's courage to live to the fullest continues to inspire me and motivates me to go on with pursuing this vision, which is to take God's message to the world through acts of kindness. That is what I hope to inspire in others.

As an ambassador of Christ, I must not live a comfortable life because God has entrusted much in people like you and me. He didn't send us to live safe lives. He sent us to live dangerously, to be bold and courageous, and to dare to get close enough to reach for our sisters' hands and grab them from the gates of hell. I believe we have a big responsibility on our hands. We are constantly intertwined with older and younger women. Therefore, we need to be conscious that when we are in the presence of older women, we are in learning mode, and when we are with someone younger, we teach. We lead by example, living our lives for Jesus.

Regardless of where you are at this point in your life, you can never be too busy for God. I encourage you to make the commitment and get to know Him on a very personal level and follow Him. It's the best decision you'll ever make.

I am not a Bible scholar, a pastor, or a pastor's wife. I am a woman who loves God with all my heart, mind, and strength. I am determined to continue on this journey, motivating other women to do what we are called to do because united we are stronger, and together we can do amazing things for His kingdom.

It's been more than thirty-five years, and with much dignity, my brother has endured many operations and strokes and struggling beyond words. Oscar never complains or asks, "Why me?" He's expressed how grateful he is that none of us (his family members) have endured his hardship. He does often wish, however, that things would have been different. He is the closest you will ever get to meeting an angel here on earth.

My brother is very much aware of how God has sustained him through his darkest moments in life. When Oscar could not walk or talk anymore, God placed people in his life to be his voice. I have often wondered and asked Jesus what lessons I needed to learn from my brother's adversity, besides the fact that we must all learn from him how to be grateful for what we have and acknowledge that we are living a little piece of heaven here on earth. No matter what the circumstance, there is always someone in a less-fortunate situation, just as there are others in better conditions. A few days after Oscar's second stroke, when he was still in the hospital, not sure if he would make it through the night, I whispered in his ear, "Gordo [his nickname], please ask God to tell you what I am supposed to learn from all your suffering."

The next morning, I had not talked to anyone yet, but I had made up my mind to quit my pursuit of launching an organization to assist people in need. The challenges had become more difficult. Because of the stroke, Oscar could not speak, but that morning he spoke words to me that have left a huge imprint in my heart forever and have been a source of strength when I am weak.

He said, "I have an answer for you—that the white flag you wish to lift as a sign of surrender you must put away and never think about quitting again. There are too many people who need help. You are to stand firm and continue walking forward, and when it gets tough, remember to take one step at a time. Quitting is not an option. Celeste-Kuri, God is with you."

I knew I needed to be bold and have the courage to continue on this path. At that moment, I recognized I had a mission to fulfill. As I gasped for air, my knees were weak, and I could barely stand, I thought; *No one knew I was giving up. How can this be?* About a minute later, Oscar began to lose the ability to speak again, yet he still managed to whisper this last sentence: "These are words from the Master."

The last sentence of the message he conveyed ignited me to instill a pact and seal it with the Holy Spirit, which was to continue on this path for as long as there is breath in me.

Not having credentials to preach is not an excuse. Moses was given a very important commission to fulfill but didn't feel he could accomplish it because communicating wasn't one of his strengths. Yet Moses was obedient. He trusted God every step of the way. Even when things became difficult, he knew he could never quit.

My heart is filled with passion to do God's work here on earth. I feel compelled to take His message everywhere I go through words of encouragement and acts of kindness, and if we need to add girlfriend stuff, coffee meetings, and shopping, so be it!

There is so much need, and we have so much to be thankful for.

Q: What will it take for you to realize you have much to offer and that the world needs people like you and me? What are you waiting for to begin a journey of self-discovery? What hinders you from making the commitment? Is it a valid reason, or are you afraid to confront your own skeletons and use this reason to hide behind a mask of fear?

Q: Have you ever met anyone who has inspired you to be a better person? Have you ever met someone who helped you realize that your life is not as bad as you thought? Is there anything that hinders you from doing something special for someone? What? What are you waiting for? List other ways you can make a difference in someone's life. Have you ever helped someone, and by doing so, they in turn actually helped you more? How? Is there someone is your life right now who you admire for what he or she does or how he or she does it? How can you be a blessing to someone today?

I know what you're thinking: *Wait! Hold on, that's too many questions!* That's the point. To take this opportunity, and use this guide to ask questions you don't normally think about. The purpose is to provoke you to reflect on the issues we usually take for granted because we may believe our ways work. Do you know the saying, "Why fix it if it ain't broke?" Or perhaps you are one who thinks that old habits are hard to break. Trying on your own hasn't worked, and uncovering yourself to the unknown scares you. Nevertheless, you may feel you are not undergoing any out-of-the-ordinary situations when in reality you've avoided the topic for so long that it's been forgotten, so you have confidence in thinking it's fixed.

The problem is that we may still be broken, and for that reason, we would rather stay as far away as possible from confronting such truths because we don't like to be confronted. We choose to wander and stay away, not realizing it's not that bad and most importantly that we are not alone. At times people feel paralyzed to take a step toward reaching out. Fear freezes them.

Many times due to the same fear and lack of confidence, countless people are afraid of committing and would rather not get involved since they believe what they have to offer isn't enough or much at all. Perhaps they believe they don't have anything to contribute, but this is a lie that stops us from going out there and doing something for those who need help! Don't let that stop you from becoming all you were created to be. It is imperative for you to know that each one of us has something to give.

Last Thoughts

Take a moment and think of the people who have made an impact in your life, who inspired you to take a stand or stay on the path that leads to honor, truth, and integrity. Doesn't this encourage you to carry on this link and begin to pay it forward? I promise it's time and effort that will be well spent! In case you haven't realized it, those who left a significant effect on you are a gift, and you can be a gift to someone—a miracle sent from heaven.

- *What left an imprint in your heart?*

Love and be kind to one another.

Serving is not just a privilege;
it's a responsibility.

Chapter 2

Oxygen to My Soul

It all began in 2006 when my sister and I visited my brother Oscar. We saw that they were in need of some help. Little did we know that experience would end up changing our lives forever!

Friends and family gathered and raised enough funds to improve their living conditions, making possible an extreme home transformation. It was an amazing turnout! Just like the show *Extreme Home Makeover,* it was awesome to see so many people gathered for this purpose. Family, friends, and the community pulled together to help a family in need, and it was such a privilege to be a small part of making this possible.

As the event came to an end, my brother said having this new place to live was like a *dream come true.* This experience changed me. I have never been the same since. Now my sister and I are dedicated to making a difference by helping one person at a time. We figured if we can bring a lil' cheer into the homes of those who are struggling, why stop here? So our journey began, and what started out as a mission became our purpose.

I believe making people happy even in the smallest things, and especially to bring hope to an individual or a family, can be life-changing! An encouraging word, a kind gesture, offering a helping hand—anyone can do this! Sometimes it's just getting informed about what's going on, or where help is needed, this way if you come across someone who may be able to help, you can quickly reach out. That is considered doing something.

Can you imagine if you were the one who desperately needed help? Wouldn't you like it if people actually cared? What if you or someone you love were battling cancer; your son just passed away; the flood took your home; you were raped; your parent was in jail; your son was enslaved to drugs; you recently were let go from your job; you were contemplating suicide; a blood transfusion infected your child with AIDS; your friend from college just found out he had Lou Gehrig's disease; your husband was kidnapped and never found; you needed a transplant to continue to stay alive; your son, a soldier, was killed in the line of duty; your son was in a car accident that left him in a quadriplegic state; or your child was taken at twelve years old and sold to sex traffickers? There are so many other terrible scenarios that exist all around us, and sometimes it's easier to pretend they don't exist. It helps us sleep better at night. There is a saying in Spanish, "Ojos que no ven, corazon que no siente." It means" Eyes that don't see, heart that doesn't feel" But it does exist! Horror stories of hunger, pain, sickness, etc., are all around us. Turning your face the other way to avoid seeing these sad truths, is easy to do. Personally, I think it's a little cowardly. Look around! You don't have to do everything, but you can definitely do something!

Can we cure the disease or bring back the deceased? No. But can we bring hope and light into these darker situations? Absolutely!

It's not always easy. Many times we hide behind a mask of fear. We have a fear of the unknown. We don't know how we can help or what we can do, and it's not because we don't want to help in any of these circumstances; it's because our fear takes over, and it can paralyze us. Next thing we know, we feel or believe that our help won't really matter. And that's furthest from the truth. It matters, and it matters sometimes more than words can say.

I have been transformed from within, and I feel compelled to encourage you to see the dire need of how much help is needed all over, and do something about it. Extending a hand to a family or individual who's going through a tough time, uplift their spirit, and encourage them with kind words, can bring hope back into their lives. As you do this, you will discover it can be like oxygen to the soul.

This has taught me a valuable lesson. Life is too short to waste it on things that are temporary. It is much more rewarding to spend time doing things that are transcendental. I know this is a journey true girlfriends in God will travel till the end of their days. I invite you; better yet I challenge you to come travel this journey. You will never be the same.

We are so lucky to live on this amazing planet, in this perfect time, surrounded by magnificent people! It's time we acknowledge and realize that we are here for a reason. What better way to express our gratitude than to extend a hand to someone in need.

Another thing I am very passionate about is relationships; after all it is the only thing we will take with us when we part from this world. Spending time with friends is priceless. When you experience God's grace and forgiveness in friendship, you have received a gift from heaven!!

So you see why I feel compelled to send this message to every one of you who is reading this, especially if you are contemplating becoming a girlfriend in God. You must travel this journey of self-discovery where no masks are required, understand the worth God has given you, and embrace your own kind of fabulous so together we can do incredible things that will change a little piece of our world!

Q: Do you now know the battles that are worth fighting for? Are you afraid to make a real commitment to God? Why? Do you recognize and acknowledge that as a follower of Jesus, you have a responsibility to serve others? What's it gonna take for you to join in on the link of giving?

Last Thoughts

If you haven't already, it's time to find a group of awesome girlfriends and together be the change you want to see in our world. Begin this transformation in your home, and then let's serve in our community, and finally let's do it with a group of amazing women who are ready to make some noise. Let's get this party started all over our world!

Chapter 3

So Much Love

How you made me is amazing and wonderful, I praise you for that. What you have done is wonderful. I know that very well. (Ps. 139:14 CEB)

Margaret Feinberg wrote this in her book *Being Yourself*:

There is no one like you. You are intricately woven and formed. You have a unique set of talents and gifts, interest and passions. God went to great lengths to make sure you were different from every other human being on the planet. And with more than six billion people, that says a lot![1]

Knowing this truth makes me so happy! Think about it—over six billion people? And He spent precious time on you and me! Yet as flattering as it is to know God loves us this much, we still want someone else's hair, body shape, career, and

---

1   Margaret Feinberg, *Being Yourself*. (Nashville, TN: Thomas Nelson, 2008), 15.

personality, and we wish for others' God-given gifts and talents without realizing we have our own set of remarkable strengths. And yet we begin to question: "Why am I like this? Why can't I be more like that?" Sometimes it can be difficult to accept our own stuff (like our short legs or tons of freckles), but it's only because we haven't fully grasped the depth of how much God loves us. What an honor to know He made us specifically the way we are and with purpose.

Gracie, my friend, is beautiful inside and out. Her composure is so lovely indeed; she is elegant and graceful. I wanted so badly to be like her. She taught me a valuable lesson. Here is what she told me which I have applied and kept close to my heart till this day. She said not to walk, talk, or act like I am in a hurry, even if I am beyond late. She explained it like this: "Visualize a little dog, a Chihuahua, to be specific. They are nervous and hyper and at times can be a bit too much to handle."

I looked at her and nodded, and with much anticipation, I said, "Yeah, go on."

There was a moment of silence, and her eyes said more than a thousand words, but she didn't even speak one. In my mind, all I heard was the sound crickets make late in summer evenings. Gracie stared back, and without her having to say anything, I said, "*Ohh, I get it!*"

As simple as it sounds, this visual was revolutionary for me! Gracie is aware of how much energy I have and knows that sometimes it is difficult to keep it contained, especially when my emotions are high in the sky. That lesson saved me from continuing to look like a crazy woman (or Chihuahua) walking as if I was being chased. Whew! Thanks, Gracie!

Q: Know any Chihuahuas? What thoughts come to mind when you see this behavior in someone? If this is you, will you take Gracie's advice?

I finally got it! I was acting like a crazy Chihuahua who probably overwhelmed everyone around me, not noticing my high level of energy needed to be toned down a few notches. At the time, Gracie's peaceful demeanor fooled me into thinking that was what radiated true conviction. I assumed godly meant quiet, sweet, and very well behaved.

My mentor was like that too, so I figured that's what it meant to be a woman of conviction, but in all honesty, I stressed about that. Often I wondered, *Do I stand a chance? Will I ever be able to reach being seen like them?* I tried to emulate that kind of attitude for a while. I felt like when I was ten years old and playing house, pretending to be the mom. I was acting and going through the motions, doing what I was supposed to, but it just didn't feel quite honest. It was exactly that—acting.

Q: Do you know a Gracie? What thoughts come to mind when you see this behavior?

As time went by, I continued to be perceived as crazy and unconventional. I'm very outspoken, and I firmly believe in transparency. I find myself constantly running into people who have an issue with this and would rather wear masks to hide. My behavior has never stopped or limited me from going after my pursuit of happiness. I knew deep within that what seemed to appear as an untamed personality actually had a purpose.

Often I asked God, "Why can't I be seen more like my very well-put-together friends?" I wanted desperately to handle myself in the same manner they did and acquire Gracie's graceful composure. I remember every time she was asked simple questions, such as, "How are you?" she'd always say in a sweet, melodic tone, "Great. Everything is incredible. My husband and the kids are doing wonderful!" Even if that was not always the case; her poise left everyone in awe. She presented herself almost flawlessly. Yes, it is a lovely trait indeed, but sometimes it can seem too perfect, and it makes others, including myself, doubt if the person is being honest.

I told her way back at the beginning of our friendship that if we were going to be good friends and I asked questions such as, "How is everything?" or "How are you doing?" she needed to answer with something else besides, "Great!" Otherwise, how was I supposed to set the tone for an honest friendship? I told her, "Better yet, how about answering with the truth?"

On the other hand, being an open book, I had a different response if I was asked, "How are you?" Well, let me just say that if I had just realized the scale showed it was ten and not five pounds I was over and I couldn't fit into my favorite jeans, oh, I'd say so, loud and clear, and without any smooth jazz tone in my voice. If my kids were driving me insane and I was thinking about placing an ad on Craigslist that read, "Free kids if anyone wants them," I'd say it, without any guilt or remorseful feelings! Pretending everything is okay can be exhausting. I am not suggesting that you should pour your heart and soul out to anyone you don't consider a friend, but in real friendship, honesty and sincerity are key factors to having that kind of freedom. That's what friends are for!

Q: How do you feel about this? Do you struggle with opening up with others? If so, why do you think it is?

The more I dug into God's *Word*, the more I understood and embraced how I was created and uniquely designed. Finding the "why" became very clear, especially when I understood God's love for me and recognized I could never be perceived as flawless. In all honesty, I don't want to be perceived in any other way except for how I am. It's ungrateful to want to be something or someone else.

Oftentimes life takes us through difficult roads. We do not always understand why we endure so much pain along the way. But I do know our faith is tested, forming stronger Christian character, and we learn lessons so that one day our lives may be a testimony, bringing hope to many who believe they are alone and feel misunderstood. The rewards are worth the bumpy ride!

When we are true to ourselves, it allows others to freely be themselves and gives a more real perspective of what Christianity is. We are not perfect. We make mistakes, our kids make mistakes, and our husbands make mistakes, but we live by *grace*; therefore, we ought to extend it too. Remaining on the narrow path instead of the wide one is a challenging journey, a constant learning and growing process, and it is absolutely crucial to stay connected to God.

Staying connected leads to spiritual maturity, subsequently helping us to distinguish between what is truly important, plus we learn to make wiser choices. (Smart decisions help us avoid making dumb ones. Wish I'd known this earlier in my life!) Another way of putting this is that we learn to fight the battles that are worth fighting, and we stop worrying about silly things like, "What are they going to say?" or "What will they think of me if ...?"

I've been there many times. In the past I've abstained from making certain choices because I was afraid of what others would think only to later regret my decision. But making wrong accusations, and conclusions, or assumptions about someone ... ladies, it needs to stop! Make sure that you do what is pleasing in God's eyes.

Remember, the world is so diverse; that is why it needs you and me! You may limit yourself from fulfilling your destiny if you don't know the extent of who God created you to be and the incredible potential you have to do amazing things. This is why I am so passionate about this—because in this truth lies the possibility of people coming together to do mind-blowing things for the community and for our world! Not knowing your potential, limits yourself from not permitting others to receive the blessing you were intended to be.

Q: Have you felt or thought at one time or another that you don't really have much to offer? Would you rather leave things as they are and avoid getting involved in something that requires you to get out of your comfort zone? Or does the possibility of making mistakes and maybe undergoing some disappointment prevent you from taking a step forward to reach out and help?

I will always be somewhat quirky and in all probability will continue making mistakes. I have much to learn, but one thing

I do know is the immense love I have for God. I love Him with all of my mind, heart, and strength. I am determined to do my part in this world. We know that reaching success takes a lot of perseverance. Mistakes equal important lessons learned. No mistakes made or not even making an effort, is the equivalent of giving up before you begin. Quitting should never be an option, especially when we are working for what we've all been called to do: To put our faith into action and serving one another. Mistakes are a part of the growing process, so it's okay to mess up. At least you're trying.

Q: Are you afraid of reaching out to someone or an organization that can really benefit from your help because you are scared to make a fool out of yourself or to make some terrible mistakes? Is it procrastination or laziness, or do you feel you are too busy?

I wish you would know sooner than later the amazing work of art you are and the potential God's given you to do great things. You are fierce, strong, and a beautiful warrior called to fight for those who can't. Let's do amazing things for the glory of His kingdom!

I had the privilege to be one of the few people with whom a friend opened up; therefore, I got to know her pretty intimately. One day we got naked with one another (metaphorically speaking, silly!), and we shared experiences from our pasts. I went first, and after hearing my stories, she figured, "What the heck? I can open up too."

When we finished that conversation, I felt closer to her than I ever had before. Once again, I witnessed how God works in ways that are beyond our comprehension. You wonder how talking about unpleasant experiences can contribute to positive outcomes. It reassures us that all people have pasts they are not proud of, but we can be transformed in Him and our pasts becomes just that—the past. Not to mention the fact that you feel accepted, even with all the baggage. You don't have to go through life alone. So glad we can count on friends.

Thankfully, my free-spirited attitude helped my friend free herself from a few chains that still had a hold on her. As fragile human beings, we are afraid of unveiling the "real us." We are scared that we might not be accepted by others, and fear rejection. We often think, *If they only knew where I've been, what I've done, or what I really think about certain things, people would think I'm the worst kind of person.* Keeping up the "I have it all together" act is exhausting and can really drain us.

I was very happy that my friend allowed herself to be vulnerable and I guess "normal" meaning that we all have stuff. Opening up to someone was not an easy thing for her to do, because of her fear. Therefore acting proper and having an attitude of "I have everything under control" is often a mask many rather wear to hide from the truth.

It was refreshing to know *she is like me—imperfect, fragile, and forgiven!* Experiencing that kind of closeness, acceptance, and unconditional love brings hope. That day was the beginning of an honest and free-of-wearing-masks friendship. When acceptance as-is exists in a friendship, it's liberating. There is no need to pretend. We say what we feel without being afraid of being judged. There is no need to walk on eggshells—and that's a great feeling! Learning about your friends' likes and dislikes is so important, and especially understanding your friends' personal outlooks in life helps make your relationships stronger. By learning to accept one another you become closer, even if you think some of their ideas or ways are a lil' cuckoo. It's a friendship where no masks are required.

Q: Have you experienced this kind of closeness with someone? Were you able to talk about the skeletons in your closet? Did it create a stronger bond between you? Or was the result the opposite? Do you have friendships where it feels like you have to walk on eggshells? If so, how does that make you feel? What stops you from telling her about this issue? Do you share the kind of friendship where you are able to be 100 percent yourself? How does that make you feel?

Unfortunately, friendships don't always turn out to be what we hoped for or envisioned. But it's okay; you take the good and discard the bad, remembering the many laughs and the great moments shared. Not all relationships are forever. Some friendships are here only for a season. Some of the beautiful friends I don't see any more left an incredible imprint in my heart, and I choose to take that with me. I am thankful we crossed paths and were in each other's lives, even if only for a season.

Gracie's undeniably graceful attitude taught me so much, just as I have helped her to not be afraid of being transparent. She is on a quest to find true freedom. We are pleased and very blessed to be on the same Jesus team. I thank God for allowing me the privilege of knowing her. Our friendship endured some turbulence, only to teach us more in depth about God's grace, love, and forgiveness. We embarked on a journey of pure honesty and self-discovery; which in turn helped us comprehend even more so, who we are in God's eyes. Today we are as close as two peas in a pod. We respect and admire one another and are very much aware how fortunate we are for second chances! God is what holds this friendship together! I love her!

When enduring difficult times, it can be so exhausting, especially when we are trying to withstand them in our human strength. These verses promise to help make you stronger; it is through His power that we can do all things. Read these great verses.

> We can endure all these things through the power of the one who gives me strength. (Phil. 4:13 CEB)

> Consider it a sheer gift, friends, when tests and challenges come at you from all sides. You know that under pressure, your faith-life is forced into the open and shows its true colors. So don't try to get out of anything prematurely. Let it do its work so you become mature and well-developed, not deficient in any way. (James 1:2–4 MSG)

> My brothers and sisters, you will have many kinds of trouble. But this gives you a reason to be very happy. You know that when your faith is tested, you learn to be patient in suffering. If you let that patience work in you, the end result will be good. You will be mature and complete. You will be all that God wants you to be. (James 1:2–4 ETV)

Q: Is it hard to believe or understand that we are to give thanks while going through a tough situation? Does that sound crazy?

Like it says in James 1:2–4, how do we give thanks while enduring difficulty such as: going through a divorce; or when finances are running on fumes; maybe you haven't found employment; perhaps there's been a cancer diagnosis; or a betrayal from a spouse or a friend? Or how do we give thanks for the loss of a loved one; witness the consequences of the not-so-great decisions our children make, and endure the heartache it brings to any parent? How can our heart be filled with gratitude? The answer is faith. No one says it's easy, but if your faith is strong, it will keep you afloat, fill you with the strength you need, and bring a peace that can calm any storm. It's the kind peace that surpasses all understanding; this can only come from Him!

Going through any of these situations can make us so vulnerable, angry, and at times we may even be embarrassed. We feel lost, and find ourselves asking, *"Why me?"* To be grateful while enduring trials is not easy to do, much less understand the why. Ask God to help you, and please hold on tight to His promises. Rest assured that He never breaks them. If you need more faith to believe, read this verse.

> But when you ask, you must believe and not doubt, because the one who doubts is like a wave of the sea, blown and tossed by the wind. (James 1:6 NIV)

Please remember that even if it seems dark, scary, and lonely, God can use everything in our lives for good. He is the only one who can turn a crisis into a blessing. This verse helps reassure us of this. Ask Him to reveal the lessons for your life.

> Know that God works all things together for good for the ones who love God, for those who are called according to his purpose. (Rom. 8:28 CEB)

These are verses of strength and hope.

Q: In your own words, what do you think this means? Can you give an example of how these verses were true in your life at one point? Can you share how you can begin to apply them to your everyday life?

I finally understood that God always had a plan for me, and now I realize why He made me specifically the way He did. More than ever, I am determined to fulfill His purpose for my life. I'm not gonna lie—the ride to attaining this truth was not easy. There were lost friendships along the way. Pain and humiliation were involved, but I never stopped trusting Him, and I knew that if I remained faithful, in due time the purpose would be revealed.

Q: Do you have a better understanding of who you are in God's eyes and what you are capable of and meant to do as an ambassador of Christ?

Last Thoughts

I figured He wired me in this way, so God is expecting me to use what's been given to me and to be genuine in everything

I do and everywhere I go. I fully recognize that all I do, I do to honor God. I encourage you to explore the depth of how He has *so much love* for you. That way you too unquestionably will want to use your gifts and talent for His glory! The world needs people like you, so how about we stop whining and/ or feeling sorry for unfortunate situations and actually *do something* instead! And remember, you don't have to do everything, but please do something! This is one of my favorite verses; it reminds me how much I am loved! Knowing this gives me strength and confidence, to do something and make a difference!

> I praise you because I am fearfully and won-derfully made; your works are wonderful, I know that full well. (Ps. 139:14 NIV)

- What left an imprint in your heart?

Chapter 4

One of a Kind

You are stunning. You were born for this moment. Don't be afraid of your strength, questions, or insights. Awaken, rise up, and dare to
realize all you were created to be.

—Lisa Bevere

Every person has their own traits, personality, and characteristics. Some are inherited from your mother and father, and some are influenced by your environment and relationships. Your unique blend makes you a one-of-a-kind part of God's handiwork, and you are uniquely qualified to help do His work here on earth. Unfortunately, from time to time we are tempted to become like someone else rather than just being ourselves. In an effort to fit in or find acceptance, we may go to all kinds of lengths to pretend we're someone we're really not. We may be tempted to act like we have it all together when we really don't.[2]

---

2   Ibid., 15. Lisa Bevere, *Lioness Arising*. (Colorado Springs, CO: WaterBrook Press, 2010), Dedication Page.

One day, a big group of my friends and family got together and went to see an amazingly fun play. As we left the theater, all of us danced and sang as if we were part of the production. We had a great time! Two years later, one of those friends told me she needed to confess something that had been bugging her for a while. I was intrigued, to say the least. To my surprise, she confessed that she absolutely hated the play; and added that being there for two hours was like utter torture. I said, "What?" and thought to myself, *Is she kidding? And you waited all this time to tell me?* (And I didn't mean because she didn't like that awesome play) It was more like a burst of, "How could you not say this before? Why didn't you just say you didn't like it?"

I felt so bad. She pretended as if she liked it, essentially because she was afraid of giving her opinion and appearing strange, being the only one who seemed to think it was corny and plain silly. It's sad not to be able to say what you think. But feeling like the oddball, I know, can be scary at times. It took a couple of years for her to finally stand firm on her opinion, and for that I am thrilled. But girls, let's not take two years to get the courage to speak our minds and express how we feel. Remember, you are unique; therefore your tastes and your likes, or your opinions, don't have to be everyone else's. Nut'n wrong with that!

Q: Have you ever agreed or disagreed to something when you felt completely the opposite? Can you think of a way to help you or a friend who may find herself in this situation?

A common mistake all of us have made, and maybe still do, is announcing new likes, such as loving a certain item, place, or thing, but in truth we don't necessarily love it. We say we do just because we've heard everyone and their grandmas say they like it, and again, we are fearful of being different, terrified of looking weird.

We can easily fall for traps such as reading certain books, which, if it weren't for the craze going on, we wouldn't have ever heard of or considered reading. Have you noticed how suddenly contemporary style is in, and everybody wants their home decorated in this way? Maybe at heart you are an *old world* décor kinda gal. Or maybe we agree on liking certain sushi restaurants when we can't stand the thought of eating raw fish, but we don't dare say it; we just order teriyaki chicken instead. Perhaps we join yoga or Zumba because everyone's doing it.

Here is a good one—trendy hairstyles. Did you notice the Victoria Beckham trend—the hairstyle that is longer in the front, shorter in the back? (Oops, that's me; I still have that cut.) Clothing items are classic to fall for, like the skinny jeans trend or the apple bottom jeans. Well, you get the point. This can apply to whatever else is trendy at the time. The fact is it's easy to go with the flow and follow trends when in reality it isn't who we are.

Q: Have you been a victim of this? Have you found yourself falling for one of these and later regretted it, like cutting your hair, reading stuff you probably were better off not reading, or whatever else you compromised or tweaked just because others have it or are doing it?

There are times when we find ourselves at a crossroad. Our emotions take over when we've been wishing for something for so long, and we can easily get annoyed or frustrated by those who acquire it before we do or already have it, and these people can be our friends. It is easy to suddenly swiftly dislike them without any real motive (except the ones we make up in our own crazy minds). In other words, we get jealous because they have what we want. And if these people should come up in a conversation, we may make a derogatory comment about them, forgetting for that moment anything good about our friends, focusing only on the negative because of the envy we feel.

I'm sure you know what I am talking about. It may be in regard to something meaningful and important, or perhaps it's a silly issue. Our conversations can sound something ridiculous like this: "Oh my, did you see what she's wearing?" (She happens to be wearing the dress you wanted.) Or we may say, "Look at her firm body" "Yeah but she spends hours at the gym. If I had the time, my body and especially my butt would be firm too"

Sometimes this happens with things we wish we could do but are more afraid of what others will think, like having a glass of wine or taking an all-girls trip. This one is classic: "My goodness, her boobs are perfect. Betcha they are not hers." Of course they are silly; she paid for them! Then there is always someone who says, "Did you hear what her husband did or bought for her? I wish my husband would do that for me." There's nothing wrong with wishing but not when we know deep inside we are saying it with spite. And we can definitely say things in a nasty way, us women can be very catty.

C'mon, girls! Are we in high school? So what if her if her body is nice and firm? It's because she works out. Well get your tooshie to the gym. And why do you care if she has a drink? How does having a drink make you feel you have the right to judge if she is a good Christian? And for those who have the luxury of going under the knife, good for them! If a surgical procedure isn't an option for us at this time (but boy do we wish we could get some stuff tucked, sucked out, and lifted), how will being unhappy for those who can change the fact that we can't? For the husbands who seem perfect, believe me, there is no perfect one! Well, of course, except for one, and I got him!

Q: Is this an issue you struggle with? Are you happy to hear when someone acquires something you've wanted for a very long time? Do you feel a lil' sting, and after you assimilate it, does it become easy to accept? Or do you feel an immediate sense of happiness for others' joy?

But the moment you find out that person is throwing a party or there is an event of any sort, you certainly don't want to be left out; you want to be included. You keep checking the mailbox, Facebook, or your phone in hopes of receiving an invitation from that person you've criticized! I know, right? That's human nature. That's you and me hon!

I've been a victim of these at one time or another. I've gone along with the flow just to feel accepted. I've given my opinion or abstained from saying what I feel and been looked upon as weird. I've criticized others and then waited for the invitation to arrive. The truth is we all yearn to feel a sense of belonging, so we do some crazy things sometimes. As silly as it sounds, we *all* have been there at least once. Is this difficult to admit? Are you saying you've never been a victim of any of these? Who are you trying to fool?

It's like when your child tells you, "*Chloe is having a party, and I wasn't invited,*" and his or her face reflects sheer sadness. It's something like that for us too, though we are older and cope differently. Inclusion somehow represents that we are important, and liked by others. Some people care more, some care less, but everyone cares to a certain extent.

However, when your identity is placed in Him, you will always feel included because God lets you know you are very important. Things that mattered before don't anymore, such as the need to be a part of the "in crowd." You learn about real beauty, not the one the media bombards us with, and the desire for plastic surgery lessens (not totally, maybe like a 5% ☺) But in all seriousness, you acquire a deeper meaning for real beauty. Beauty is so much more than perky butts or perky anything. A person who goes out of her way to put others' needs first is beautiful. Someone who fights for justice is beautiful; someone who cooks a meal for a sick person is beautiful. The list can go on and on. You learn to focus on the things and people that matter. People who help you grow and help draw you closer to His purpose. Overall it benefits you by becoming a genuine follower and true disciple, someone who walks the walk and talks the talk, not only in theory but in practice!

You have your own traits, personality, and characteristics. You are a unique blend that makes you a *one of kind*; you are qualified to help do His work here on earth, and that is absolutely awesome!!

Change your hearts! And show by the way you live that you have changed. (Matt. 3:8, easy-to-read version)

Last Thoughts

You are awesome, and you rock. Don't waste any more time trying to be like someone else. God made you specifically the way He did with a purpose. If you aren't sure what that is, I encourage you to begin the journey of self-discovery and learn of the beauty that lies within you. In addition, learn what you are meant to do here on earth. Discover your purpose.

> You are stunning. You were born for this moment. Don't be afraid of your strength, questions, or insights. Awaken, rise up, and dare to realize all you were created to be.
>
> —Lisa Bevere

- What left an imprint?

Chapter 5

Embrace Your Own Kind of Fabulous!

I t's amazing how we can talk with other women and find we have so much in common. God created us with a *one-of-a-kind* mold. Though we may look, act, or sound alike, we are all different! Even identical twins are uniquely distinctive. We can, however, be identified by one or two of four fundamental types of personality or temperament; there is no one individual who is exactly the same as another.

Understanding the different personality types equips us to be better friends; so that we learn how to manage some of our irrational friends—including you and me.

In her book *Being Yourself*, Margaret Feinberg writes the following:

> Each of us has a unique personality. While numerous books and articles have documented

the differences between personalities, many can be identified in four fundamental personality types.[3]

The temperament names are kinda strange and not easy to pronounce, Sanguine, Melancholy, Choleric, and Phlegmatic, (I know, right?) and the meaning isn't related to what the word sounds like. Stay with me, I promise it will make sense. Knowing this gives a clearer idea of why those around us react differently to certain situations. While one friend may freak out simply at the thought of an earthquake, another is calm, cool, and collected while experiencing the earth shaking. We can easily get frustrated, upset, and even hurt by the reactions of some our friends. At times we expect to receive a response that is not within the person because it's not who they are, or how they think. Recognizing these differences teaches us not to take things personally. Also, it helps you to plan accordingly for when you get together with a friend. While for some having fun is going to a place where there is music and dancing, others would rather enjoy lunch and a movie or any other quiet place to savor a more intimate conversation.

Q: Do you enjoy a loud atmosphere? Do you prefer quiet? Or are you okay with both?

Which one is better? They both are! They're simply different. No personality or temperament is right or wrong. So tell me, what do you think your friends say about you?

---

3   Margaret Feinberg, *Being Yourself*. (Nashville, TN: Thomas Nelson, 2008), 17

Q: Are you the life of the party, but can easily forget which weekend the party is on?

Q: Are you a born leader whose bossiness can sometimes get in the way?

Q: Are you the easy going, cool and relaxed friend, yet at times find it difficult to make up your mind?

Q: Or are you a deep thinker and a detail-oriented friend who tends to overanalyze things?

Let's see if you can identify your personality type and those of your close friends.

Carrie made an important appointment for Mary and herself at 9:00 a.m. Carrie is a woman who takes pride in her punctuality. Mary picked up Carrie at 8:00. Off they went, but Mary quickly noticed she had forgotten her purse:

> Mary: OMG, I just realized I forgot my purse!

> Carrie: Are you kidding me? It's 8:14!

> Mary: I have to go back and get it. It will only take a few minutes!

> Carrie: A few? Ha! I know your "few" minutes! (She screamed inside her head, *why can't she ever be ready on time?*)

After retrieving Mary's purse, they quickly got back on the road; suddenly the light started flashing a warning that the gas tank was almost empty. There was a gas station at the next exit, but instead of stopping, Mary continued driving:

> Mary: Uh-oh, someone forgot to put gas in my car! That's okay, we can make it; the light just turned on.

> Carrie: Someone forgot or you forgot? Oh my goodness, we can't be late! But you better stop and get gas; we don't want to risk it and make this situation worse...

> Mary: Don't worry, we can make it! (Inside her head she said, *Calm down, take a chill pill! Oops, I just passed the exit.*)

Suddenly the car began to make a weird noise. It slowed down and started to shake, rattle, and ... no mo' roll. (Wah, wah, wah.) Mary thinks to herself, *Okay, I'm dead. She is going to kill me! Good-bye, world!*

Q: Can you relate? Which person do you identify with? How does this make you feel? What can you learn from this? Let's discuss another situation.

The girls planned a happy hour for Friday at 5:00. It's Friday at 3:15 p.m., and Brenda receives a phone call from Ana:

> Ana: Hi, Brenda. I just wanted to let you know that there's been a tiny change of plans.

Brenda: *Change of plans!*

Ana: Only that we changed the time to an hour later. Oh—and to a different restaurant.

Brenda: A different place? (Inside her mind she asks, *why can't they just stick to the plan?*)

Ana: Relax; it's no big deal. (Her inside voice says, *why does she have to make such a fuss? Whatever ...*)

Brenda: Okay, fine, see you soon. (Inside she says, *I wish I would have known this sooner. I am not dressed for that restaurant. I **really** dislike changes!*)

Q: Can you relate? Which person do you identify with? How does this make you feel? What can you learn from this? Here is a different scenario.

Nikki and Dani meet at the assigned place to drive together. After greeting each other with great excitement, Nikki asks:

Nikki: Where do you want to go? What do you feel like doing?

Dani: Anywhere is fine. I don't really care.

Nikki: Give me an idea of what you feel like.

Dari: Whatever is okay with me.

Nikki: Do you wanna go eat something? Are you hungry? (Inside she thinks, *C'mon, help me out a little!*)

Dani: Sure we could go grab something to eat, or we can wait whatever. I mean, I could eat ... or not.

Nikki: What do you feel like, Japanese, Italian, or Mexican?

Dani: Either, I will have whatever you'd like.

For some, this can drive you nuts! Others, however, consider this type to be easygoing and great company.

Q: Can you relate? Which person do you identify with? How does this make you feel? What can you learn from this?

This is the last illustration: An exciting conversation with four friends takes place about a getaway weekend trip. They've been looking to spend quality time together. All of it sounds amazing, but it seems to be just conversation. Planning it—well, that's a different story. It takes initiative and work. Two days later, this is what happens:

Bianca: I called a few hotels, and after carefully exploring our options, I made the reservations at this great place. The cost will be X. Ready?

Sandy: Wow! I didn't know we were that serious. I thought it was just conversation, it sounds amazing, but ...

Bianca: But what? We talked about it; you were so excited. What's the problem?

Sandy: No problem, it's just that ...

Bianca: What?

Sandy: It sounds great. Can we try moving the reservation to this hotel? (Inside: *Shoot, I wanted to stay at the Hilton because I have points there!*)

Bianca: No, this one is just fine.

Sandy thinks, *OMG, why does it always have to be her way?*

Some people would consider this too bossy, while others are grateful to have someone close who takes initiative.

Q: Can you relate? Which person do you identify with? How does this make you feel? Is it easier to praise your friends' strengths, and can you be more patience in the areas of weakness each of us have?

Last Thoughts

Understanding yourself better and those close to you will help avoid misinterpretations and misunderstandings. By nature we are quick to act on how we feel; and without doubt take our emotions on a rollercoaster ride. Many times we don't understand our friends' responses or ways of handling certain things. They may not make any sense to us. So the sooner we discover and become aware of how they are wired, we learn to expect less, and many times receive more. Learning to identify your strengths and weaknesses guarantees a higher success rate in any relationship. I invite you to embark on this journey and *Embrace your own kind of fabulous*!

- What left an imprint?

Chapter 6

Fun, Sassy, Feisty, or Sweet Chick

The Sanguine (or Fun-Guinni)

Girlfriends with the sanguine personality type (or as the giG calls them *fun-guinni*—cuter, right?) are the fiesta people! And if there is no fiesta, they can easily make one for you! They are very high in energy and love people! Ms. Popular is their middle name. Because of their outgoing personalities, it's easy for them to have conversations with anyone. As a matter of fact, starting one with a stranger is exhilarating to them.

Fun-guinnis are easy to spot. When they walk into a place, they will definitely be heard or seen; they speak with their hands, and their eyes can have a conversation of their own. When they tell you a story, they explain it with such detail that it feels like you're watching a movie. They laugh a lot and sometimes a bit much! These people will quickly make you feel at ease and can fill an empty moment with a funny story. Fun-guinnis treasure friendship. Therefore, making friends comes very easily. A fun-guinni will often demonstrate her appreciation for her friends by regularly making sure her friends are aware that she is thinking of them. Awe sweet!

Wait, there's more, and it's not all sweetie pie stuff either. Because of her enthusiasm and charisma, she is great in front of people, leading meetings, and motivating others. When you receive an e-mail or a letter from her, you know it's from a fun-guinni because of the emphasis on the points she wants to make by adding a ton of exclamation points! Writing is easy, sending the letters ... ay, ay, ay, that's a different story.

Though they are dynamic and fun, fun-guinnis have a down side. Uh-oh, here we go. A fun-guinni tends to procrastinate; for some, procrastination can be their last name. She needs to be stimulated with new activities or meaningful endeavors. For example, she can start a project or task that seems fun but can quickly become bored and begin to look for a new project to take on. Fun-guinnis put their foot in mouth quite a lot! This happens because fun-guinnis talk a lot! It's easy for them to dominate conversations and finish sentences for others. A fun-guinni is usually not very organized ... okay, not at all! She writes notes commonly on napkins, on the back of an envelope, or on any piece of paper she can find. Punctuality is not one of her strengths. But rest assured that whenever you are with a fun-guinni, there will never be a dull moment!

Q: Is this you? Do you embrace being a fun-guinni? Why or why not? Is there something you would like to change?

Word that best describes the sanguine: Popular

Q: What interesting things did you find out about yourself? What interesting things did you find out about your closest friend or friends?

The Melancholy (the giG Call Them Sassy-Choly)

Sassy choly girlfriends think a lot, sometimes while they're thinking they sorta stare at you, and might make you believe you are being ignored; when all it is, is that their thought process works differently. Sassy choly types are known for their more in depth analyzing ways. They are known to be geniuses, which make them excellent at finding solutions or answers to problems that take patience, and a lot of intelligence to resolve.

They are also very artistic. Sassy-choly types are scheduled individuals. They actually use the features in their smartphones, and they set alarms! Wow, right? They live by their daily planners. (The fun-guinnis find super-cute ones with matching pens, but when they need to use them, they can never find them.) When starting a project, they won't rest until it is finished. If a sassy-choly offers to do something, you can rest in knowing it will get done! They are cautious individuals when it comes to letting people into their hearts.

Sassy-cholys are loyal and devoted friends. Most have a dry sense of humor but can make you laugh with comments that weren't intended to be funny. Generally they are quiet and easily moved by heartfelt situations. They ooze compassion, and they usually love to drink tea. (Okay, I made that up, ☺ but only because most of my sassy-choly friends love tea. It's not a rule.)

They can, however, be very negative, finding fault in many situations. For instance, if their personal things are not in the order that makes sense to them, it can drive them *nuts*! (*Note*, just because it makes sense to them doesn't mean it's neatly organized.) It frustrates them when individuals don't consider tardiness to be a lack of respect. (Is it? I'm joking!) Therefore, they get angry easily if someone is late to an appointment, and if their plans should change—holy moly! Not a good thing! They tend to be pessimistic, often seeing the glass as half-empty. And because they are perfectionists, it's easy for them to fall into gloominess if people or plans don't come up to their expectations. Also, it's easy for sassy-cholys to take their thoughts on a voyage of their own, travelling to unnecessary places, causing them to get perplexed about things that haven't even happened.

Nice to know you can always count on the reliability of your sassy-choly friend. When they say "yes" it doesn't mean, maybe, it means yes!

Q: Is this you? Do you embrace being a sassy-choly? Why or why not? Is there something you would like to change?

Word that best describes the melancholy: Perfectionist

Q: What interesting things did you find out about yourself? What interesting things did you find out about your closest friend or friends?

The Choleric (Known to the giG as Feisty Go-Leric)

Go-lerics are known for being leaders. They are born wanting to take over and be the boss. (The rest of us learn to be leaders.) Also, they are recognized as Ms. Practical and sometimes Ms. Bossy. These women are no-nonsense kind of gals. A go-leric is the one you call when you want to get the job done. They have goals for everything and constantly preach to others about the importance of setting them. They don't get distracted very easily, unlike the fun-guinnis and sassy-matics. If you find difficulty getting to one place or need to talk to a person, go-lerics find a way to make it happen.

In situations where decisions need to be made *pronto,* it is always good to have a go-leric around. They can easily get you out of a difficult situation. If you are caught in a position where you haven't got a clue what to do, they will act as if they know exactly what they are doing until someone who does know comes along. They are energetic and accomplish many tasks at once. They really like e-mail because it cuts to the chase, avoiding extra blah-blah-blah about things they often find unimportant. In addition, they react quickly to situations.

Like the fun-guinni, because of their confidence, they are also good in front of people. However, they can push people instead of leading them, easily taking the fun away from getting things done. They are often more interested in getting results than worrying about emotional well-being. So if you find yourself in need of a kindhearted, gentle moment, a go-leric is probably not the person to call. If you are ever in need of a tender moment, I strongly advise you to carry the number of the most phlegmatic friend you have. Go-lerics can easily detach from emotions, seeming cold at times. And when you need an explanation or opinion, they can make you feel inadequate because of their lack of patience. But remember, if you are ever in need of someone to tell it like it is, call a go-leric!

And anytime you need help in getting something done ASAP your feisty-go-leric is the one to call. They are awesome do-ers!

Q: Is this you? Do you embrace being a go-leric? Why or why not? Is there something you would like to change?

Word that best describes the choleric: Leader

Q: What interesting things did you find out about yourself? What interesting things did you find out about your closest friend or friends?

The Phlegmatic (We Call Them Sweet-Matic)

Last but never least of the four temperaments or personalities is the sweet-matic. Sweet-matics are awesome because they are very easygoing; it's great to have friends with this temperament. This type however, is one of the most difficult to spot. They can be very chameleon-like, mixing in quite gracefully in any given situation; except don't ask them to speak in public or give orders.

Generally they are very easygoing, relaxed, peaceful, and agreeable human beings. They are great listeners, and they have a lot of compassion for others. Those with this personality type often find themselves engaged in conversations with people they just met, and hearing about their life stories. They exude a "you're safe with me" appearance. Talking to them always feels very comfortable, and somehow it feels *familiar.* Sweet-matics are great friends, making them excellent company, and they are often described as very nice. There is a sweet essence about them.

They can, however, be unenthusiastic and indecisive. This personality type also can be oversensitive at times, needing constant reassurance from those who love them. It's easy for sweet-matics to take comments personally when they aren't directed toward them at all. Go-lerics and sweet-matics can easily become exasperated with each other due to their opposite ways. While one's patience is mostly always on the edge, to the other, patience is a gift.

It takes a long time for sweet-matics to make up their mind about most things, and from time to time, it may require a lil' push in the tooshie to get them to try and do something new or different that may require them to leave their comfort zones. They are not too keen on anything that involves a lot of effort. Sweet-matics are all about comfort and relaxation. That's just how they roll.

And when you spend time with your sweet-matic friend, simply "chillin' like a villain!" (Do people still say this or did I just give away how old I am?)☺ It is very likely that you will be in a relaxed and comfortable mode, laughing and merely having a good'ol time!

Q: Is this you? Do you embrace being a sweet-matic? Why or why not? Is there something you would like to change?

Word that best describes the phlegmatic: Peaceful

Q: What interesting things did you find out about yourself? What interesting things did you find out about your closest friend or friends?

More Questions—Let's Answer Them Together

Q: Did you find your temperament? Which is the predominant one? What others are you a mix of?

Q: Name a few important things you learned from this.

Q: How can you use your temperament or personality to bless other people?

Q: Is there an area of weakness you need to work on? Which one?

Q: What did you discover to be your strength?

Q: Did you find this to be helpful? What new things did you learn about your friends' strengths and weaknesses?

Q: How can you use your and your friends' temperaments to bless others?

If you surround yourself with friends with different personalities, imagine the possibilities of the lessons we can learn from one another. The world already makes distinct separations because of our differences. Let's *not* be like that! God fashioned us all differently to enrich our lives. We need each other, and the world needs different personalities to deliver God's message. Otherwise He would have made robots. Let's embrace our differences and use them to help strengthen us instead of pushing others away. God wants unity! Diversity helps us grow. Accepting this truth is a mark of maturity.

Last Thoughts

So whether you are a *fun, sassy, sweet, or feisty chick*, God created you with special attributes, so that we may complement each other. By using our gifts we will shine even brighter as we walk on this journey of self-discovery; uplifting one another in areas of weakness. Being a source of strength and encouraging each other; and together be a blessing to others in our own unique and distinctive way.

The amazing people from the Old Testament, such as Peter, who was a sanguine, Mary, a phlegmatic, Abraham, a melancholic, and Paul, a choleric, were ordinary people who did extraordinary things. You can do the same! Whatever you do, always remember to embrace your own kind of fabulous, because you, my dear giG, are absolutely magnificent!

- What left an imprint?

Remember to always be

your own kind of beautiful!

Chapter 7

Triggers that Make You Say, "Hmm"

No test or temptation that comes your way is beyond the course of what others have had to face. All you need to remember is that God will never let you down; he'll never let you be pushed past your limit; he'll always be there to help you come through it. (1 Cor. 10:13 MSG)

Okay, so I seriously have no excuse whenever the "Sale" signs appear. First Corinthians is very clear: there is no temptation God will not give us a way out of. If I try using the excuse, "The sales were too good to resist," I know I am only trying to convince myself of something that is absolutely not true. No matter how cute the item is, I have to remember 1 Corinthians, 1 Corinthians!

Through the years, I've noticed there are things that are pretty obvious I was weak in, and shopping was one of them!

Whether it was buying shoes, pearls, or a leopard scarf, I felt shopping was an escape from reality. I loved going to the mall and immersing myself as if nothing else existed; I'd browse for hours and then buy things I didn't actually need. It was as if I wanted to fill a void.

Something triggered the need to shop. The question is— what? This is why finding your trigger is necessary. Triggers can be simple things like your spouse annoying you, unpaid debt, cattiness, and even an unkempt house. Are you like me, thinking yes to all of the above? Yeah, I know, but think deep and find what really makes you angry—angry enough to cause you to fall and sin.

Margaret Feinberg wrote in her book that one day she was asked a question she had never been asked before: "Is there a trigger in your life that causes you to sin?" *Wow, right?* That's a question that makes you say, "Hmmm." I don't know about you, but I have never thought of finding a trigger before. Interesting, right? After doing a lot of soul searching, I found that the answer for me is *inconsideration. This is my trigger.* As for Margaret, she found that what triggered her was lack of sleep. Here is what she says:

> I realized that the thing that causes me to sin the most was simple, lack of sleep. When I don't get a good night's rest, I tend to be short with people and less forgiving; I'm more critical and selfish. I feel cranky and rather than think of those things that are good and true and beautiful, I find myself distracted by anything uncomfortable or negative. I also tend to over-eat for energy boost throughout the day. Once I recognized that lack of sleep was a trigger

point for sin in my life, I began to pray that God would use this realization to transform me.[4]

After recognizing your trigger, the next smart step is learning to deal with it. I always have trouble handling inconsideration; it is not easy for me to hear people say or do things without empathizing with the other person's situation. When someone is going through a circumstance that is causing pain, sadness, discomfort, or any other feeling, even if it sounds crazy to us, it isn't to them. Therefore, treating the issue with dignity and respect is important; sometimes comments are said unintentionally.

I understand this all too well. I've had my share of mishaps, but to say things knowing full well they can hurt someone just because they may seem funny? Not cool. Or when a person needs a little assistance—perhaps carrying groceries or helping someone who is handicapped or disabled—If someone walks on by because getting out of their comfort zone and making the effort to help seems tedious, that is difficult for me to witness.

I remember one day, I was in line at the border waiting to cross to San Diego, and there was a man in a wheelchair selling gum as a means of making a living. That already is sad in itself, but then someone was kind enough to buy some candy from him. With much effort, he wheeled himself closer to the car to give the man in the truck his candy, but the man tossed the money a little too hard as he drove off, and the money landed on the ground. As much as the man in the wheelchair struggled to get it, he just couldn't.

---

4   Ibid., 47–48.

You could see the man's face fill with anguish and desperation, and even though it was only change, he tried with all his might to pick it up. I remember my blood boiled because people saw this and would not help. I was too far back in line, and alone in the car. I couldn't just leave the car. But how can people see this and not do anything? This irritates me too, people who make a mess and leave it, expecting others to pick it up. It's pure lack of consideration. It takes effort to help. Some people either haven't been taught that it's the right thing to do, or rather not assist, because they simply don't care. I want to yell and say, "Where are your manners? Or, do you know the meaning of consideration?" Ayayay! (That's oh my goodness, in Spanish!)

Inconsideration pretends it doesn't see and struggles when asked to help. Ahhh! That makes me very angry! And once I am angry, no, my clothes don't rip and I don't turn green, but it's easy for me to fall and sin. I tend to answer with an inappropriate tone or make facial expressions and unkind gestures that speak louder than words. (That's what my husband says!) I may even say a word or two that I probably shouldn't; thoughts I don't want invade my mind. The list can go on and on, and if someone is inconsiderate to me, I can have a pity party. Suddenly the words *always* and *never* are emphasized in anything I say. I begin to make up senseless stuff like: *Doesn't anyone care? They **never** help me. Why am I being taken for granted? It's **always** me who has to do everything.*

After I've reacted to the trigger, and when my emotions take over, the fun begins ... I go to the mall and shop! But I make unwise decisions about my purchases. (When I get my statements is when I realize this, and it's not so fun after all.) I go home with a new item (or a few) but unresolved feelings, and it's because I wasn't able to detect the trigger to control it.

I ask God to use this realization and help transform my thought process whenever I encounter a situation that can lead me straight to … the mall. Knowing I'm being triggered beforehand helps me by giving me the opportunity to handle the situation better. If we let the warning light go from yellow to red, it can easily become a bigger deal. It is important to detect your triggers and deal with them accordingly. Imagine a bowl of fresh, juicy fruit. If one piece of fruit gets spoiled, little by little the rest of the fruit spoils too. That's how our thought process works; one bad thought can lead to many bad thoughts. Scripture reminds us that we need to continuously cleanse our hearts so our thoughts are pure.

> Brothers and sisters, continue to think about what is good and worthy of praise. Think about what is true and honorable and right and pure and beautiful and respected. (Phil. 4:8 ERV)

Q: How can this verse help you next time you catch yourself ignoring the yellow light trigger alerts?

Here's another version of that verse:

> Summing it all up, friends, I'd say you'll do best by filling your minds and meditating on things true, noble, reputable, authentic, compelling, gracious—the best, not the worst; the beautiful, not the ugly; things to praise, not things to curse. Put into practice what you learned from

me, what you heard and saw and realized. Do that, and God, who makes everything work together, will work you into his most excellent harmonies. (Phil. 4:8–9 MSG)

Q: How can you divert your thought process from twisted thinking to thoughts worthy of praise?

Look what it says in Luke:

> Good people have good things saved in their hearts. That's why they say good things. But those who are evil have hearts full of evil, and that's why they say things that are evil. What people say with their mouths comes from what fills their hearts. (Luke 6:45 ERV)

This verse is a mirror to all of us, especially when we've said some awful things and try to justify them by saying, "I promise I didn't mean it." This verse shows us that what we say is what is stored up in our hearts. If we store good, good will come out and vice versa. Basically, if we don't constantly cleanse our heart, it can easily get filled with dirt. As a result, our thoughts become muddy. Our words then lead to actions that we end up regretting. A purified heart lessens (not guarantee) the likelihood of saying hurtful words.

Q: Can you think of a time when this verse proved its point?

Being aware of the triggers that can cause us to sin helps us to guard ourselves; *this is why* knowing yourself is so important.

Q: What areas of sin are you particularly prone to? Is there a trigger in your life that causes you to sin? Why do you think it's important to be aware of your triggers?

Sin can have a powerful hold on you, but God is almighty, powerful and sovereign, and can help you overcome anything!

> As long as you did what you felt like doing, ignoring God, you didn't have to bother with right thinking or right living, or right anything for that matter. But do you call that a free life? What did you get out of it? Nothing you're proud of now. Where did it get you? A dead end. But now that you've found you don't have to listen to sin tell you what to do, and have discovered the delight of listening to God telling you, what a surprise! A whole, healed, put-together life right now, with more and more of life on the way! Work hard for sin your whole life and your pension is death. But God's gift is real life, eternal life, delivered by Jesus, our Master. (Rom. 6:20–23 MSG)

Q: In what areas of your life have you felt as if sin has controlled you? Is there something that hinders you from taking the escape route? In what areas of your life have you felt like you've overcome sin through God's strength? Can you explain in your own words what this verse means? What do you think death means in this verse?

This lesson was derived from 1 Corinthians 10:13, which says God does not give us more than we can bear. Next time you are tempted and find yourself caught in a trap, remember God always provides a way out. I encourage you to ask Him to reveal the way for you to escape.

Q: Is there something that hinders you from taking the escape route? What is it?

Last Thoughts

Take a moment and think about the *triggers than make you say, "Hmm."* Pray for God to reveal what triggers you. Ask Him to use this realization and help you transform your thought process when you encounter a situation that can lead you to sin.

Remember, no test or temptation that comes your way is beyond you. God will never let you down.

- What left an imprint in your heart?

Chapter 8

Loved and Accepted As-Is

If you hold on to my teaching, you are really my disciples. Then you will know the truth, and the truth will set you free. (John 8:31–32)

It was April of 1994; I had been married for eight years. Our marriage was enduring problems (that's putting it mildly). I figured, why not seek help and learn to handle my husband? (Clearly he needed a lot of help.) Being the excellent wife that I am, I went to a course/seminar for self-development, personal growth, insight, and awareness (yeah, yeah, whatever), which, to my surprise, took me for a ride I will never forget. There were moments when I literally looked around thinking; *There must be a hidden camera somewhere, because this has to be a joke*! I kept waiting for someone to say, "Smile, you're on *Candid Camera*," and hoped for Ashton Kutcher to come out and say, "You've been punked." (Unfortunately, Ashton was about seven at that time, so not a chance!)

I stood in front of approximately fifty or sixty people without being able to say a word. I silently stood there, my arms down and to the side. In addition, I was not supposed to make any facial expressions either. *Ha, good luck with that!* As I stood there quietly and waited for the exercise to begin, the anticipation had me shaking at my knees. But I never let a soul know I was so nervous and a lil' afraid. When I heard that the exercise consisted of becoming aware of how people perceived me, I thought, *Oh, piece of cake. This will be easy, probably fun too!* They undoubtedly would say things like *cute, fun, happy ...* I never could have imagined what happened next. People stood in front of me, one by one, looking directly into my eyes, and began to yell these words over and over:

"**Hypocrite, fake, cynic, clown, hypocrite!**"

All I could think was, *Are they kidding?* So I smiled and tried to be cute, but they would yell, *"Clown, cynic ..." Why are they saying this?* I thought, smirking and trying to look away. I could not believe my ears or how much I had paid for the seminar, for that matter, just so I could be humiliated! *Give me back my money! Security!*

Soon after I committed my life to Christ, it became clear what I was supposed to learn in the course I had attended a few months earlier. Hearing others calling me a hypocrite, among other names, was a wake-up call. (Not fun!) It was then that I acknowledged I indeed had been a hypocrite for years. I had pretended to be something or someone I was not to fit into the circles where I thought I belonged.

I understand hypocrisy well and can detect it very easily. You know the saying, "It takes one to know one." Being around fake people has been a big issue for me, and it was one of the biggest obstacles I encountered early in my walk with Christ. I went from being a hypocrite to becoming a legalist and essentially judging everyone. I completely lost the concept of empathy. I didn't show or express any compassion for anyone who didn't know Christ or for those who already knew Him. I was oblivious.

So what's worse, a hypocrite or a judgmental witch? Both are equally awful! Then I learned what God says about love in truth; it is to accept others as-is. God loves us as we are—only He loves us too much to leave us the same. It doesn't mean you must go along with others' lifestyles or viewpoints. I'm sure you've heard that God hates sin but not the sinner. Besides, when we encounter any situation, mostly we judge based on what we see or hear. Too often we hear only one side of the story, forgetting it takes two to tango. It's hard to really know the whole story. How many times have you encountered an incident where you thought something about someone and later found that what you thought all along was far from the truth? Therefore, we shouldn't be so hard on people; instead, let's first give the benefit of doubt and always extend grace and be kind.

Q: How many times have you acted like something you aren't only to fit in? How many times have you judged based on what others tell you about someone? What have you learned about judging without really knowing the truth? Can you think of an incident of either of these scenarios?

Only with God and His grace can a person be transformed. It is up to each individual to want to change. We can only show our sincere kindness; Jesus takes care of the rest.

A few months ago, I had the opportunity to talk to a woman I had judged pretty harshly concerning motherhood based on what I saw. I apologized for making derogatory comments about her choices with her children. She is a tough woman; therefore, it's not easy to approach her. She hasn't had it easy in life, so to protect herself, she reacts defensively, and her tone of voice is pretty intimating. She's a single mother of four who works very hard to offer her kids a better opportunity in life.

Though I find that an admirable trait, still, I wasn't very fond of the decisions she made concerning her children. A few minutes into the conversation, she began to cry as she expressed how sorry and guilty she felt for making some of her choices. She conveyed how she wished she could have been more present for her children, but she felt there was no other way. Her priority was to make sure her children had food and shelter. I said to her, "If only I had known this before." We cried together and reconciled our differences. The past can't be changed, but the present can. I now will defend her and any other single moms out there, because unless you are a single mom, you can't understand the choices they find themselves having to make. They can seem plain careless, but in reality sometimes they really don't have any other choice.

Not being aware of my actions, I realized I was acting as if I were a perfect mother who was never late to pick up my kids, never missed a soccer game, and especially never said to them, "Wait a minute, hon, I'm busy." Wow, it was so enlightening to get a glimpse of my own actions and of how I seem to forget I am no one to judge, especially when it comes to the situations single moms endure. It was a powerful lesson, and I am glad I learned it.

I do not sit with the deceitful men, nor do I associate with hypocrites. (Ps. 26:4 NIV)

I don't run around with troublemakers. I have nothing to do with hypocrites Ps. 26:4 ERV)

Ouch! Thank God for His mercy and grace! Let's read what it says in Matthew about being a hypocrite.

Don't pick on people, jump on their failures, and criticize their faults—unless, of course, you want the same treatment. That critical spirit has a way of boomeranging. It's easy to see a smudge on your neighbor's face and be oblivious to the ugly sneer on your own. Do you have the nerve to say, 'Let me wash your face for you,' when your own face is distorted by contempt? It's this whole travelling road-show mentality all over again, playing a holier-than-thou part instead of just living your part. Wipe that ugly sneer off your own face, and you might be fit to offer a washcloth to your neighbor. (Matt. 7:1–5 MSG)

Q: What do you think about Matthew 7:1–5? Have you ever been in a situation where you were stuck seeing only the speck in your friend's, brother's, husband's, etc., eye but didn't see the timber in your eye? Have you ever met anyone who acts holier than thou, so much so that it's uncomfortable to share things because you feel you'll be looked upon as weird or worse? Do you have the courage to share?

Pretending is never good, regardless of the situation. Jesus is all about the truth. Let's read what these two verses say in regard to truth and grace.

> To the Jews who had believed him, Jesus said, "If you hold on to my teaching, you are really my disciples. Then you will know the truth, and the truth will set you free." (John 8:31–32 NIV)

The truth sets us free.

Q: Do you remember an incident where you pretended or flat-out lied about something or someone, and it was eating you up inside, but when you told the truth about it, it was like a ton of weight had been lifted? The truth sets you free. Are there things you don't like about yourself that you are committed to work on and improve on? Are there certain things about yourself that you once didn't like but you've learned to appreciate? Name two.

When Jesus came, He was full of grace and truth.

> The Word became a man and lived among us. We saw his divine greatness—the greatness that belongs to the only Son of the Father. The Word was full of grace and truth. (John 1:14 ERV)

We've all pretended to be or acted like someone at one time or another; it's much easier to make believe than to face the truth, especially when our reality seems somewhat dark. We are accepted as is. Hypocrisy is not being truthful or real; it's hiding behind a mask. Pretending leads to desolation. Making others believe to be something that we are not, is sad. Remember, we are accepted as is.

I'm sure there's an Ellie in your group of friends or acquaintances. She is the one who has done it all and been everywhere, and she knows pretty much everything! Someone will be talking about certain experiences, and she will always say she's been there or done that, but you know it's not true. It's one of those situations where your blood can easily sizzle with frustration because you know the truth, but you choose to remain quiet, and extend compassion instead. It's clear she hides behind an "I-know-it-all" mask. Sadly the truth is, most of the time she knows very little or nothing at all about the subject; but she rather pretend in order to feel accepted.

After a while these people begin to believe their own lies. They speak with certainty, when you know it's all fabricated. One thing is clear, they are afraid of seeming ignorant, so pretending becomes a better choice. It is okay to say "I don't know." You don't need that mask!

Q: Do you know an Ellie? Are you an Ellie?

It is perfectly fine to say you don't know about certain issues, and it is even better to continue to be a student of life. Learning from other people's experiences and viewpoints can be very enlightening. It is okay to take off the know-it-all mask and show others the real you. People like genuine people.

Jen Hatmaker wrote in her book *Girl Talk*: "There is no place more fake these days than the church. I'm sick of it. He [God] would prefer an honest mess over a pretty lie every day of the week."[5]

I don't know about you, but I've made a few messes along the way. I am so grateful that Jesus is so patient with us. The Bible talks about many stories of men and women with ordinary skills who made extraordinary choices, leading them to miracles that changed the history of mankind! They made a ton of mistakes along the way, yet they had a commission to fulfill. That ordinary person can be you! God wants to use us.

Q: When you think of finally being you, how far along in the process do you think you are on a scale of one to ten, with ten being the closest? What areas do you struggle with in becoming who you truly are?

A mask is the shield one uses for protection. It makes it easier to be accepted and included in groups that require meeting certain criteria. This clearly limits the possibility of anyone ever getting to know the real "unmasked" you.

Being open and transparent can cause some people to get uncomfortable, whether they are afraid of being detected or simply because people are not used to speaking or hearing the truth. Many would rather be PC (politically correct), going along with whatever is said, even if it's against their principles, or stay quiet and not risk it. Some would rather omit the truth because they dread the tension it might bring

5   Hatmaker, *Girl Talk*, (Colorado Springs, Colorado, NavPress 2007), 62.

to the conversation, as well as into the relationship. Instead they choose to hide behind a *smiling mask*, assuming that speaking the truth may not be received in the spirit in which it's being said or that they will not be respected for their personal point of view.

It's a rare thing when you find people who are not self-conscious, always saying what is on their minds. At times these individuals may lack a filter when they speak or share their opinions, but it's truly refreshing to witness. I know a few women who are totally comfortable being as authentic as it gets. They speak their minds at all times and dress in their own eccentric style. It's cool to see this. But I have to say; not very many people can appreciate their uniqueness. They can be seen as a bit odd, and others do not easily accept their often-unconventional way because people are not accustomed to things that are different. This is when we ought to put on the glasses that help us see how God sees and focus on the important things, like their kind hearts. Next time you are in the presence of someone you consider to be different, I challenge you to see beyond and look into her soul.

Q: Have you experienced being open and transparent? What was the outcome? Are you in a place where you would rather wear a mask because it's more comfortable or safer? Do you know someone who is constantly hiding behind a mask? Which mask? How do you feel about this? Do you know someone who is totally genuine? How does being around her make you feel?

Jen Hatmaker says, "We make a calculated decision not to speak openly because we attach a higher value on keeping the peace than on authenticity."[6]

We attach a higher value on keeping the peace than speaking freely or standing up for someone and/or giving our honest opinion. What are we so afraid of? We are afraid of being authentic and being seen as a feisty chick.

Q: What do you think about the following statement: "We attach a higher value on keeping the peace than speaking freely or standing up for someone"?

Q: Do you consider yourself to be someone who would rather stay quiet or speak out when someone is bashing your friend? Why do you find this to be important or not?

I often find myself defending those who are dear and near to me—and even those who are not! Personally I believe it's a matter of justice and integrity. Justice is doing what is pleasing in God's eyes. Speaking harshly about people we supposedly call *friends* doesn't sit right with me. Now don't get me wrong—it's *not* like I am this perfect human being who never says anything bad about anyone, because I am certainly not perfect. I have made the mistake of talking about someone before. But I try not to. I work on this on a daily basis. I keep it present in my conversations, so that I don't slip and fall into this. It's not fair to say stuff about people when they are not present. Preventing this practice takes training, but like everything, if you keep at it,

---

6   Ibid., 128.

eventually it will become a habit. I guess defending others can be a fault or a virtue depending on your viewpoint.

When someone says something derogatory about someone I love, someone I don't know well, or even about someone I don't know at all; I strongly dislike it. It's not easy for me to hear when a person is being attacked with offensive or destructive comments because it can be very damaging. Most of the time people base things on what they hear, think, or see; but not necessarily on facts. My instinct is to defend, automatically becoming an advocate for the other side. Annoying those who wish to stir up the conversation, expecting to hear similar comments or simply agreeing with what's being said. We all like it when others go along with our thoughts, but I think everyone deserves to be given the benefit of the doubt. Maybe this time, those you are talking about have changed! Maybe their old ways and habits finally came to an end. Perhaps, it was never true what so many said about him or her. I firmly believe in second chances. I was given that chance; I got a do-over. These people you may refer to in a negative manner could have an incredible purpose to fulfill. Why are we going to add to the awful comments that can only bring them down? There is too much of that going on in the world already. Let us be different! It's better to develop compassion, and practice extending grace.

Q: Have you ever been with a group of people in which you weren't strong enough to abstain from participating in a conversation, maybe even agreeing to unkind comments about people you call friends; perhaps adding to or deducting from the truth; volunteering unsolicited information just to feel a sense of belonging or to make others believe you think like they do; or possibly even using false flattery? In other words, have you participated in gossip? Or have you noticed you defend the other person by not just refraining but actually stopping the conversation? Are you okay with being seen sometimes as a feisty chick who tries to make sure others are reminded there are always two sides to every story? Or would you rather stay quiet and appear serene and well composed to keep the peace? Why or why not?

How awful, right? And even more so when we pretend we've never been there. Not long ago one of my best friends and I were discussing an incident that happened with a mutual friend of ours, and the more we talked, the more annoyed we got. We left feeling yucky about ourselves because she is our friend. The next day we saw each other, we made a pact, which was that we would not let each other speak negatively about a friend, even if we were annoyed, frustrated, or both. And if one of us were to start, the other would say a word that reminded us of the pact. Though it may sound silly, it works. It helps when you are accountable, teachable, and correctable. Our code word was *ding-dong*. I know! What does that have to do with anything? Ding-dong? Really? It sure throws us off and makes us laugh, which in turn stops us! Mission accomplished. Try it!

Q: Have you ever been so annoyed or angry with a friend that whenever the chance comes up, you vent about it?

These three awesome verses are great reminders. Keep them close to your heart, and always fight this war with the sword that cuts deep—the Word. The more you learn about the Word, the more you'll remember that it is a powerful weapon that can fight against anything!

> Without wood a fire goes out; without gossips, conflict calms down. (Prov. 26:20 CEB)

> Gossips reveal secrets; don't associate with those who talk too much. (Prov. 20:19 CEB)

> Destructive people produce conflict; gossips alienate close friends. (Prov. 16:28 CEB)

If we'd realize there is spiritual warfare going on all the time, we'd prepare and be stronger to fight against it. Unfortunately, we are unaware of it. Here is another sword to help you fight the spiritual battle:

> And that about wraps it up. God is strong, and he wants you strong. So take everything the Master has set out for you, well-made weapons of the best materials. And put them to use so you will be able to stand up to everything the Devil throws your way. This is no afternoon athletic contest that we'll walk away from and forget about in a couple of hours. This is for keeps, a life-or-death fight to the finish against the Devil and all his angels. Be prepared. You're up against far more than you can handle on your own. Take all the help you can get, every weapon God has issued, so that when it's all over but the shouting you'll still be on your feet.

Truth, righteousness, peace, faith, and salvation are more than words. Learn how to apply them. You'll need them throughout your life. God's Word is an indispensable weapon. In the same way, prayer is essential in this on-going warfare. Pray hard and long. Pray for your brothers and sisters. Keep your eyes open. Keep each other's spirits up so that no one falls behind or drops out. (Eph. 6:10–18 MSG)

There are things we know aren't good for us, the Devil makes them sound exciting, trying to lure and entice us with his manipulative ways. We easily get caught up in believing the lies we hear from others or the lies within our own minds. *It's okay. It's not that bad, this is the last time. How can this be so wrong when it feels so right?* Ladies, be careful; sin disguises itself in various ways and can take numerous forms or behaviors that can look very appealing. It makes the prohibited look desirable. Perhaps this happens in simpler things, such as believing you can afford certain things when you can't, or maybe you think it's okay to live a lifestyle that isn't for you. Perhaps you chose the wrong person to share life with! Or maybe it's having immoral friendships, knowing full well you don't agree with the other person's habits. This can go as far as pursuing someone else's spouse. These are all fabricated lies we fall for.

Q: When was the last time you tried to justify a story or a point you made, maybe even a supposed joke you said, but you know deep inside it was a lie? What can you do differently?

We've all stumbled on things that look very attractive, like a beautiful array of sexy shoes—*danger zone!* Doing or saying things we shouldn't leads straight to feeling guilty and shameful for having participated in something we know full well is wrong. It doesn't matter how spiritual people may be—deep in their hearts, they know their wrong decision will lead to trouble. However, experiencing the moment becomes more enticing, making it difficult to choose what is right. We believe the lies we tell ourselves, like, *Just one more* or *This is the last time, I promise.* I strongly advise you to protect yourself at all times with the armor of God.

This can also be common in habits. I used to have a bit of a mouth on me when I was younger (way younger, like two years ago; I'm joking), and saying bad words was the norm. I actually used bad words to fit in, to look and sound cool, and to be like the rest of the crowd. At the beginning of my spiritual walk, I even said them so people would not think I was a prude. As time has gone by, and as my spirit remains on a quest for continued renewal and cleansing, the use of this kind of language has diminished, though I must confess not totally. But I'm working on it.

There is one specific word that lashes out, especially when I hit myself, when I remember something important, and for sure when I pass my exit on the freeway (which happens quite often). It's the caca-poo word. I try very hard to modify it by saying, "Shut the front door" instead, but I know better.

Q: How many times do curse words slip out when you hang out with friends who use this kind of language? Are you strong enough to not let your friends' habits influence you? Maybe you fall into drinking a bit more than you wanted, or smoking, over-shopping, or so many other things. Have you stopped and taken the time to acknowledge the change in behavior when you are with certain people? Check yourself next time.

A woman I knew surprised me with a phone call one day. She told me how sorry she was because she had talked very badly about me. I was distraught but immediately said, "It's okay." I thought, *I guess she didn't mean it, right? I mean, why else would she feel the need to confess? Or maybe she did, but now regrets saying things.*

She replied, "But you don't understand—I said *very* bad things!" She even asked if I wanted to know what she said and to whom she said it.

I figured, what's the point? I preferred not to know. This would keep me from being embarrassed or worried about seeing anyone who could have possibly heard something negative about me. In truth, I did often wonder what she said and to whom. I was sure she fell into a trap as she participated in a conversation and went along with the rest of the people as they probably gossiped, and it wouldn't surprise me if it was with other Christians! What? Christians? *Yes!* This phenomenon happens with all people, regardless of their beliefs or convictions. So what's the point of this story?

We're human, and as a result, we are fragile; and without doubt, all of us at one point have been the *gossip girl*. Can you say you've never done such a thing? I know I have. Committing our lives to God can't guarantee it won't ever happen again, but asking God with an open heart to help transform our old habits and align them with His can definitely help, slightly minimizing the errors we make.

If you're neither protected nor strong enough to be with others with whom you might easily fall into sin, be wise and choose the smart way out. Temptation is always lurking, and the Devil looks for ways to divert us from the truth, especially in the areas where he knows we are weak. No doubt he wants to derail us from our convictions, morals, and values, and he hungers to seduce us to try things for the first time and like them! We can easily go back to our old ways. Look out; he knows your weaknesses and will use them against you. Temptation disguises itself in all different shapes, colors, and forms. *Be careful!*

> No temptation has seized you that isn't common for people. But God is faithful. He won't allow you to be tempted beyond your abilities. Instead, with the temptation, God will also supply a way out so that you will be able to endure it. (1 Cor. 10:13 CEB)

I was first introduced to Christianity through a growth group. One of my dearest friends at the time invited us to her home, and the six couples attending were all there for the same reason—to try to save what was left of our marriages. Some of us went all in on what many call the "God thing," and I was one of them. I was only one signature away from finalizing my divorce. All of the couples in the group were broken and a mess, ready to give up yet holding on to the last thread of hope. I guess we figured we could say anything; at that point, what could we lose?

From the beginning, we were very open, especially me. We accepted each other as-is and felt safe knowing we all had some ugly in us, no exceptions. This created a very special bond between us. And as we began to mature and know

God, we applied the lessons we learned, and our lives began to transform right in front of us. It was fascinating to witness. Most of us remained close friends and rescued our marriages; we made it!

I believe in being genuine and unmasked, errors and all! I guess I don't know any other way to be. It is liberating to speak the truth and nothing but the truth. Even if others disagree, it's admirable to stand firm in your convictions and stay true to yourself. Hiding behind a mask can be risky. You may get comfortable, forget who you truly are, and inhibit yourself from living a life of freedom.

From the beginning of my walk with God, I was open, honest, and transparent. Anything else seemed odd or hypocritical in a sense. People want to learn about the Word and enhance their lives but keep on hiding behind their masks.

Your story potentially can be someone else's life jacket, helping in a powerful way to set others free. If you dare to unveil yourself and discover the real you and cause mess-ups along the way, it's okay; God's got your back. Remember, you are *accepted as is*!

Looking back, as crazy as it sounds, having been called *hypocrite* among other names was actually a good thing for me. Though it was an exercise to convey what people perceived and not what they actually knew to be true, it made a huge impact in my life. I'm not gonna lie—it was dreadful, humiliating, and painful, but I can't deny it since I discovered it was true. And quite honestly, it's helped me to be able to detect those who hide behind a mask. It also has given me the ability to have an extra dose of compassion for them because I was once there. Thankfully, I have been set free! I heard someone say once, *"Be yourself; everyone else is already taken."* It's not only liberating, but it's also the right thing!

Lisa Bevere says, "God doesn't love us the same, He loves us uniquely!"[7] This journey helped me become the person I am today. Extending grace and accepting others as-is is one of my main strengths, and it has become a mission for me to live up to. I have faith in the power of the Holy Spirit. I trust that love transforms, and I believe in second and third chances. I am very thankful for the amazing God we love and serve. He is compassionate, and He forgives and loves unconditionally.

Last Thoughts

If you have not permitted others to know you, I encourage you to take baby steps toward opening up and allowing others to know the no-mask, fabulous you because you are amazing! Your story is the hope someone is waiting to hear to set them free. It's time to throw away the mask! Regardless of where you've been or what you've done God longs for you to open your heart and make a real and honest effort to unveil and discover your true self. I challenge you to begin this journey or to continue to stay on this path until you reach the freedom you and others long to obtain. Remember, you are not alone on this road to finding true authenticity.

You, my darling, are awesome and are *accepted as-is*—only God loves you too much to leave you the same! His love transforms!

- What left an imprint?

---

7   Lisa Bevere at a *Godchicks Conference* (Los Angeles, CA, 2012).

Chapter 9

Diversity Is a Beautiful Thing!

We are all different—in our ethnic backgrounds, the ways in which we were raised, our different walks of life, and certainly the way we deliver God's message. Pretty awesome, right? Finding diversity in everything is a beautiful thing!

I joined a group of lovely Christian women for all the right reasons but stayed for the wrong ones, only to realize that when you stay in a place to impress someone other than Jesus, the outcome will never be what you expect or hoped for. I learned a ton from the leader; she is an amazing woman who I have a lot of respect for, and it was a privilege to have worked by her. Being a part of that group gave me the opportunity to meet wonderful people and witness many miracles.

However, I dreamed of many new ventures I wanted so badly to take on, and I knew it wasn't going to happen if I stayed. I understood that their ministry is already established, and that's great. But I wanted to launch new projects that weren't necessarily a part of their mission, and this was the first "*aha*" moment I encountered where I was convinced that diversity is essential in our lives. This organization touched thousands of lives and I am honored to have been a part of it.

There comes a time when God calls us, and it's up to us to listen. I am happy I listened and pleased we have diversity in leaders for every kind of ministry. The way I see it is, we are all sailing on the same ocean, just in different ships. We may all take different routes, yet we are all navigating toward the same direction. Toward Jesus and His truth! Our goal is to serve others and take God's message to the world, and no one particular ship or method is better—just different. It was time for me to spread my wings and fly. Leaders want the same thing in the end, which is to help lead others closer to Jesus and ultimately follow Him so one day we will meet again and dance together in heaven!

Q: Have you heard the voice inside that tells you to get involved and do something but are afraid of taking on this challenge? What holds you back from this calling?

We know that the New Testament sums up the Ten Commandments in two: 1) Love God with all your strength, mind, and heart, and 2) love your neighbor as your love yourself. Essentially, follow Jesus and serve one another.

Serving is done through acts of kindness. Some deeds are big, some are tiny, but any act of compassion is always big in God's eyes. You can help in many ways, whether you are helping the less fortunate, feeding the hungry; advocating for justice; volunteering and giving your time to those who truly need it; going on a mission trip; freely giving words of encouragement; going that extra mile for someone you love or for someone you don't know; opening your home and offering Bible study; providing hospitality to someone in need; preaching by example without having to quote the Bible; displaying sacrificial love; putting others before yourself; offering someone a break; listening; smiling; hugging; mentoring; or doing many other things that can bring cheer to someone who has lost hope or simply is in need of a hand.

To some people, none of these come easily, but I tell you the truth: everyone has something to give or offer! Perhaps it's lending your house for a fundraising event. It can also be simple things like taking the time to inform yourself about issues that are going on in our world that desperately need solutions because you may know someone who knows someone who is the answer to a bigger problem. Buy a ticket to anything where you know the funds are for a good cause, even if you can't go. That counts as helping or doing something.

Q: Is this you? Can you see clearly how something so simple can be a huge help? Will you make the effort to learn more and get more involved? Why?

Have you ever thought you would be fine if you only had one eye, one arm, one leg, etc.? We can certainly survive, but the truth is every part of our body is important, and we are grateful to have all of our body parts. This principle applies in ministry as well. Each one of us has a calling, and with our unique gifts and talents, we are able to complement one another, making any group or team stronger.

I get very enthusiastic about this because I have witnessed so much competitiveness and even cattiness between strong women who lead or help in organizations. It's frustrating, and in all honesty, my heart aches when I see this kind of behavior. If we could only understand that we are on the same team. If we put our immature ways and pettiness aside, we could do amazing, mind-blowing things together for His kingdom! Why can't we understand that we need each other? We have been called and entrusted with bigger things than our egos. This is not about you or me. It is, however, about putting ourselves into the shoes of the person who's struggling beyond words. We must be compassionate and do what we can for others. I know we can't do everything, but we can certainly do something.

I like the illustration of exercising. For instance, do you enjoy the pain of sore muscles, sprains, stiffness, etc.? The effect of doing two hundred squats is particularly painful, and we certainly feel it when we sit and pee—*ouch!* The stiffness and the pain in the rear (literally)—oh wow! Yet we enjoy it at a certain level because that soreness signifies that our muscles are being worked. Nevertheless, even though we know exercising will help improve our health and make our bodies look better, more often than not we get lazy. We become complacent and figure, *It's okay. Life is too short to abstain from such guilty pleasures as In-n-Out and Haagen Dazs.*

In my culture, abstaining from enchiladas, tacos, and carne asada burritos is plain brutal. But the voice inside says, *Celeste-Kuri, if you continue to eat fatty foods, your cholesterol level will go up.* I gaze at my plate; see the carne asada taquitos with rica salsa right in front of me, and knowing full well the cholesterol level and especially my thighs will show the consequences. Do you know what I say? *No big deal, I'll start eating better mañana.* This is nuts, yet we do this all the time. Do you remember the saying, "A *minute on the lips, a long time on the hips*"? Though we know this to be true, we ignore it!

Q: Have you been in this place before, knowing the truth but ignoring it?

We experience the same thing in our spiritual lives. We recognize and acknowledge that following God is the right thing to do, nevertheless we get lazy or complacent. Sometimes we are even afraid to commit because we think our lifestyle will change drastically, and the fun will be cut in half. Plus if we know there is an area of sin we struggle with, we feel guiltier. Instead of reaching out for help, we hide. It's easier to run away from the problem than to run to God for help. We make the problem bigger than God, but never forget that God is *bigger* than any problem and bigger than anything!

Sometimes it is a little threatening or intimidating to see people who act or seem too good or kinda *goody two shoes.* Believe me, there is no one who is too good. We are *all* sinners and fall short of the mercy and grace of God! But I can completely understand how this attitude may drive some people away instead of drawing them nearer to God.

One of the many reasons why I love my church is because our pastor doesn't hide the fact that life is full of struggles. It makes all of us feel better knowing he too has them. He makes it clear that marriage is hard work. It also helps to know that every now and then, you may feel like wanting to give up, it is part of the process, but the key is not to! Giving up should never be an option. However in order for this to be somewhat easier, it is crucial to stay connected. Be accountable to others, and give God a real honest chance.

We must make sure that no matter what is going on, we put God first and foremost in our lives so we can have a true opportunity to come out triumphant. Our pastor explained how he struggled with commitment when he first became a Christian years ago. Hearing this is so encouraging because it fills us with hope and we can relate.

Q: Have you ever met people you admire but they seem too good, like you could never reach their level? What about meeting people who seem pretty faithful and firm in their convictions but struggle like you and me? What are your thoughts?

God gives us opportunities to make the necessary modifications in our lives, which are far more beneficial to each one of us, yet more often than not we choose not to follow. Why wouldn't we choose His way? Could it be because we don't take the time to learn about what God wants for us and from us? It's easy to make wrong assumptions.

I can't count the number of times people have assumed things in regard to what they think Christians can and cannot do. Some are so far from the truth. I was there too. I used to think Christians were a lil' weird. Someone close to me said; "in that religion they don't allow people to wear make-up, you can't even wear pants, and you definitely won't be able to have a drink. Are you sure you want to be a part of that cult?" A good friend of ours we've known for ever wasn't sure to invite us to his daughter's quinceañera, because he thought or *assumed* we couldn't attend parties. As for me, I figured that if it wasn't Catholic, then it must be a cult. It's ignorance, and not because we are dumb, but because we truly don't have a clue.

For those of us who are parents, we know what is best for our kids, though our children don't always agree. Our love for them is so profound, and as parents, we desperately want them to succeed and do great in life, but mostly we want them to be happy. Imagine that times a million. That's how God loves us. If Jesus' teachings and principles are way better than ours, isn't it logical to want to follow His ways instead of ours? So why the heck don't we? Much has to do with the fact that we are too stubborn, naïve, and ignorant to align our lives to His, but in all likelihood, almost always it's because we are afraid of committing to what is uncertain, unclear, too strict, boring and a totally unexciting lifestyle. If this was the truth about being a follower, do you honestly think I would be here today, convinced that God is the only way?

Q: Were you ever afraid of committing to become a true follower? Why? How did it change? How do you feel now? In all truthfulness, do you believe this lifestyle is boring and will limit you from many things? How?

This voyage begins with the desire to make a change, and then you get the courage and the adventure begins, thereafter staying consistent to finally accomplish your goal. After seeing the incredible results of constant exercising, you ask yourself, "Why didn't I start sooner?" When you choose to follow Jesus, your life will show the fruit of the Holy Spirit and radiate the joy within you! Looking back, it only seems like you wasted precious time. Begin your journey today, and if you've been on this journey for a while now, rise and awake! Years will come and go, and you'll wonder why you waited this long. Begin to sow today to reap the fruits tomorrow. Discover your purpose, serve, and be yourself. You are a gift to someone.

God's love is the music, and life is the dance floor. So dance and sing. Get up, and do your thing! C'mon, be bold. I dare you to ask Him to show you things you've never imagined or known before.

> Call to me and I will answer and reveal to you wondrous secrets that you haven't known. (Jer. 33:3 CEB)

There is no one right way to have a personal relationship with Jesus, just as there is no protocol we all must follow in serving. Let's love and be kind to one another.

Therefore, it doesn't matter how you dress, if you speak in a particular way, if you have tattoos, or furthermore, if you're traditional or completely the opposite. What matters is to take His message to the world by doing acts of kindness. Embrace being different, and let that unite us, not divide us. Remember, no one style is better than another. Diversity, girls, diversity! Find the church or growth group that helps you develop a stronger relationship with God and brings peace to your heart, but especially find a place where you will learn about the Word in a practical way that makes sense and can easily be applied in your life.

Maybe it's where the music touches your heart, or perhaps you relate to the person preaching, when you are reminded how people can change. Find a place where you can experience His truth in your life. Once you find it, you will know!

Q: Have you ever been to a church where you found it more comfortable than another? What factored into your viewpoint? Have you ever been criticized for the church you attend? How do you handle it? Have you been criticized for your beliefs and convictions? How do you handle it? Have you criticized other people's beliefs and convictions?

Can you imagine if there was only one defined way to serve, preach, or teach? Nowadays there are churches that are more radical about certain things, such as speaking in tongues, laying hands on people, etc. While it may cause some not to go back again, it could be the perfect place for others. Some like a nosier service and some enjoy a quieter sermon. Diversity!

Q: Have you ever attended a church that was so different from what you expected or were used to that it actually made a huge impact in a positive way? How?

Q: Have you ever attended a church that was so different from what you expected or were used to that it actually turned you off?

If you were invited by a friend to attend either a growth group or a church, even if the outcome was not what you anticipated, please know his or her intentions were good. Only good friends invite you to church. Keep that in mind.

In the Bible we read many stories of how ordinary people were used tremendously by God, each with their own uniqueness. The best part? They were people like you and me, and they made a huge impact in history.

Finding a diverse group can be a wonderful thing. Every individual is an incredible asset, bringing something new, something fresh, something you hadn't thought about. Women from different backgrounds and walks of life come together to create an unbelievable dream team!

If we all liked the same things and did the same stuff, we would miss out on so much. For instance, can you imagine if we always had chocolate lava cake? Scrumptious, right? But what if we didn't give key lime pie a chance? And both are lip-smacking! In addition, what if you only saw action-type movies, such as *Mission Impossible*, and missed out on watching *The Notebook*? Oh no, heartbreaking! And the best analogy for this is what if you only wore flat shoes and limited yourself from wearing high-heeled, fabulous ones? That would be catastrophic! Diversity is a beautiful thing!

Check out diversity:

Q: What is your favorite store?

Q: Are you a sweets or salty type of gal?

Q: Do you prefer the beach or pool?

Q: Dog or cat?

Q: Casual or fancy?

Q: Vanilla or chocolate?

Q: Skittles or Starbursts?

Q: Day or night?

Q: One or two friends or bigger groups?

Q: Law & Order or Modern Family?

Q: Hamburgers or tacos?

Q: PC (politically correct) or straight to the point?

Q: Winter, spring, summer, or fall?

Q: Comfort or suffer the pain for beauty?

Q: Hershey's with almonds or plain?

I believe it is indispensable to recognize your likes and dislikes to better identify your strengths and weaknesses.

Q: What new things have you learned from others who are opposite of you? And what have you learned from those who are the same?

You and I are pieces of a puzzle ready to be discovered and positioned in a specific place. The puzzle cannot be completed until all the pieces are found. As part of giG, I feel compelled to challenge each one of you to learn what is your piece of the puzzle? We have a big responsibility on this earth. The sooner you understand the profound worth God has given you, the quicker you ought to use your gifts and talents in your own unique and distinctive way. Together we are able to inspire, serve, and teach others. Don't be afraid of your strengths. Unleash them for His glory! I feel so fortunate to know and be a part of the amazing women who are bold and courageous and are committed to running the race toward making a difference in our world! I want so desperately to encourage you to do a few things as we conclude:

1) Recognize that you are a beautiful child of God, with amazing talent, and understand He's called you to do incredible things!
2) Realize and acknowledge the need in our world, and help us bring hope into the lives of the many who are enduring hardship.
3) Understand the importance of joining in on the link of giving. Connect with a group that is working on life-changing projects, join a growth group in your church, or simply support your friends who are involved in an

organization that brings relief to those in need. Commit to something that will impact lives. And if you think your gift is not much, it is! We help take care of His children and rest assured He will always take care of ours.

4) Remember, in this walk with God, you may be the pinky finger, but we need that finger too! Start with volunteering in smaller tasks, and gradually move into bigger responsibilities. God is adamant that we let Him teach to us what He wants to teach through us.

5) Remember not to focus on the differences in styles of fulfilling our purpose. Regardless of our organization, church, or group, we are all on the same Jesus team. Therefore let's exalt one another's strengths to help each other shine brighter and make the team stronger. Cheer each other on, and support your giGs' endeavors. Diversity is essential. Let it unite us, not divide us.

Q: Do you know the depth of God's love for you? Do you know that you have incredible potential to do great things? Do you realize it takes courage to go out of your comfort zone to take the first step?

It's time to do something that will leave an imprint in someone's life, whether you join a group or help a friend out.

Q: What will it take for you to begin a journey that serves others? How can you exalt your friends' strengths? How can you be a true cheerleader and help or promote your fellow giG sisters, endeavors, and events or life-changing projects? What can you do to help make other people's dreams become a reality?

Take a chance, and learn to discern the voice that asks you to go out of your way and do things that are not always comfortable but can make a huge difference in someone; for you the outcome may be ordinary, but to the other person it may be extraordinary!

Being who God created you to be is a significant calling; you are a beautiful work of art with a story ready to be told.

Last Thoughts

I hope this gives you a new perspective of who you are in God's eyes. Remember, He created you with a specific plan. There are countless people who are not able to walk or talk; who have a voice but can't be heard; and whose hope lies in people like you. They wait desperately for someone to be their arms and their legs—their correspondents. You are the hope they dream of. Ask God to reveal His plan for you, and align your ways to His. Remember, there are people behind you and ahead of you who wait for someone exactly like you, and you can lead them to the greatest gift of all … Jesus! Now get to work!

We are all different—from our ethnic backgrounds, the ways we were raised, even in our different walks of life, and certainly in the way we deliver God's message. Diversity is a beautiful thing!

• What left an imprint in your heart?

I dream ...

I dream of changing a piece of our
world. I dream of bringing a little
bit of heaven here to earth.

I dream ...

Together we can help change lives.

Dream *big*!

As a girlfriend in God, I commit to this pledge.

I, _____, fully understand the immense love God has for me. I am aware that I have been given gifts and talents, and I want to use them to bring even more meaning to my life, leaving a legacy of imprints in the world.

I commit to find my strengths, acknowledge my weaknesses, and with God's help, transform them so I reach my maximum potential and become the woman God created and called me to be. Also, as of today, I will no longer live a comfortable life. I will become bold and courageous, and I promise to go out of my comfort zone, risk living dangerously, make changes, and take chances on the things that matter. I will accept and love others without judgment. I am committed to making a difference in someone's life.

I will volunteer, starting first at my church. I will join a cause and help with at least one life-changing project, but most importantly, I pledge to be a giG, a girlfriend in God, which means supporting my fellow giG sisters in their endeavors, being the true friend I now know I can be, and giving the gift of God's love to everyone, dancing and singing everywhere I go.

Take the next right step, sign up and register, and receive information on how to continue to stay on this journey! Plus you will get to meet other amazing girlfriends who share your vision, and mission!! Awesome!!

Signature   Date

Invite a friend to join this link of giving! Hope to see you soon! xoxo

Welcome to the giG, girlfriends in God.

We are an amazing group of twenty-first-century women who are serious about strengthening their relationships with God, building stronger and true friendships, and making a difference in the lives of others.

Girlfriends, let's get this party started. Let's witness miracles together. A sense of humor is crucial for this adventure. You are now officially a part of a group of women who are committed to making life better for someone!

Keep on rocking, and don't forget to wear your party shoes!

The giG, girlfriends in God, will meet annually to share our stories of transformation. Please stay tuned for giG upcoming events.

Once a giG, always a giG

www.the-gig.org and www.sendmefoundation.com

Workbook

Welcome, girlfriend!

Let's begin. You can choose to answer a few or all of the questions. Each one takes turn. To hear others thoughts and opinions can be very refreshing.

To keep each one accountable, a petition box is a great idea. Everyone puts their name in a piece of paper and places it in the box. Each one takes a name at the end of class, and commits to pray for them that week.

These questions may seem unusual, but remember, the purpose is: 1) for us to get to know you and 2) for you to get to know yourself better.

Describe your mood right now in one, or up to three words ...

Introduce yourself in fifteen seconds—*name, marital status, age, children, pets,* and *work.* Focus on you ...

Write down why you are here and what you hope to accomplish from this giG, and place it in the box. They can be read aloud without saying who wrote what. Get a more truthful reason for what each person hopes to accomplish. The idea is for the hostess to save them and at the end of the entire session, read them again and check if each person's desire was accomplished.

Let's begin. You can choose to answer a few or all of the questions. Each person takes a turn. It is enlightening to listen to others' thoughts and opinions; it refreshing to realize you are not the only one who feels or thinks strange things sometimes. ☺

From one to ten, ten being the highest, grade your happiness.

What's missing?

What makes you smile? Name a few things.

What do you dislike? Name your pet peeves.

Tell me two or three things you really enjoy doing.

What is a smell you love and why?

Write about something you've been postponing but wish you could do today.

How does someone win you over?

From one to ten, ten being the highest, grade the following:

Spiritual life   _____
Marriage   _____
Relationships   _____
Friendships   _____
Serving others   _____

What are your hopes and dreams? What steps are you taking toward reaching them? If you aren't taking any, why not?

If you could do anything in the world (there was no family, no job, nothing holding you back), what would you do?

What would be your dream job?

Tell me a cause that is dear to your heart. Why?

Do you serve or support a cause or an organization? Do you help out or volunteer in church?

Yes No

If not, are you interested in participating in life changing projects? Circle the answer:

Yes   Not really   I wish but can't at   Ask me again later
this time

Tell me about yourself. Who are you?

How do you think people perceive you?

How do you wish to be perceived by others?

Pick a name from the box. That is your soul sister. Give her your petition, and commit to pray for her all week.

Are you ready to begin a change?

Be the change for the
generations to come!

Are you ready to rock this world?

Introduction

The Journey That Got Me Here

Q: Have you fully understood the depth of God's undying love for you? Do you completely understand that His love transforms? Have you taken your broken relationship to the Creator of relationships? Have you tried His way and put your way aside? What do you want to teach your children about relationships? Have you learned what is truly important in life? What?

Q: Do you now know the battles that are worth fighting for? Which ones? Why? Are you afraid to make a real commitment to God? Why?

Q: Do you recognize as a follower of Jesus that you have a responsibility to serve others? What's it gonna take for you to join in on the link of giving?

Chapter 1
What's It Gonna Take?

Q: What will it take for you to realize you have much to offer and that the world needs people like you? What are you waiting for to begin a journey of self-discovery?

Q: What hinders you from making the commitment? Is it a valid reason, or are you afraid to confront your own skeletons and you use this reason to hide behind a mask of fear?

- What left an imprint in your heart?

Chapter 2
Oxygen to My Soul

There is so much need, and we have so much to be thankful for.

Q: Have you ever met anyone who has inspired you to be a better person? Explain:

Q: Have you ever met someone who helped you realize that your life is not as bad as you thought? Explain:

Q: Is there anything that hinders you from doing something special for someone else? What? What are you waiting for?

Q: List other ways you can make a difference in someone's life. Have you ever helped someone and by doing so, he or she in turn actually helped you more? How?

Q: Is there someone is your life right now who you admire for what he or she does or how he or she does it? How can you be a blessing to someone today?

- What left an imprint in your heart?

Chapter 3
So Much Love

Q: Do you know any Chihuahuas? What thoughts come to mind when you see this behavior in someone? If this is you, will you take Gracie's advice?

Q: Do you know a Gracie? What thoughts come to mind when you see this behavior?

Q: How do you feel about this? Do you struggle with opening up with others? If so, why do you think this is?

Q: Have you felt or thought at one time or another that you don't really have much to offer? Do you rather leave things as they are and avoid getting involved in something that requires you to get out of your comfort zone? Or does the possibility of making mistakes and undergoing some disappointment, prevent you from taking a step forward to reach out and help?

Q: Are you afraid of reaching out to someone or an organization that can really benefit from your help, but you are scared to make a fool out of yourself or make some terrible mistakes? Could it be procrastination or laziness? Or do you feel you are too busy?

I wish you would know sooner than later the amazing work of art you are and the potential you have to do great things. You are a beautiful warrior called to fight for those who can't. Let's do amazing things for the glory of His kingdom!

Q: Have you experienced this kind of closeness with someone? Were you able to talk about the skeletons in your closet? Did it create a stronger bond between you? Or was the result the opposite? Do you have friendships where it feels like you have to walk on eggshells? If so, how does that make you feel?

Q: What stops you from telling her about this issue? Do you share the kind of friendship where you are able to be 100 percent yourself? How does that make you feel?

We can endure all these things through the power of the one who gives me strength. (Phil. 4:13 CEB)

Consider it a sheer gift, friends, when tests and challenges come at you from all sides. You know that under pressure, your faith-life is forced into the open and shows its true colors. So don't try to get out of anything prematurely. Let it do its work so you become mature and well-developed, not deficient in any way. (James 1:2–4 MSG)

Q: Is this hard to believe or understand? Giving thanks while going through a tough situation—does that sound crazy? Explain:

> But when you ask, you must believe and not doubt, because the one who doubts is like a wave of the sea, blown and tossed by the wind. (James 1:6 NIV)

> Know that God works all things together for good for the ones who love God, for those who are called according to his purpose. (Rom. 8:28 CEB)

These are verses of strength and hope.

Q: In your own words, what do you think this means? Can you give an example of how these verses were true in your life at one point?

Can you share how you can begin to apply them to your everyday life?

I praise you because I am fearfully and wonderfully made; your works are wonderful, I know that full well. (Ps. 139:14)

Q: Do you have a better understanding of who you are in God's eyes and what you are capable of and meant to do as a girlfriend in God and as an ambassador of Christ?

- What left an imprint in your heart?

- What can you do to pamper yourself this week?

Chapter 4
One of a Kind

You are stunning. You were born for this moment. Don't be afraid of your strength, questions, or insights. Awaken, rise up, and dare to realize all you were created to be.

—Lisa Bevere

Q: Have you ever agreed or disagreed to something where you felt completely the opposite? Can you think of a way to help you or a friend who may find herself in this situation?

Q: Have you been a victim of this? Have you found yourself falling for one of these and later regretted it, like cutting your hair, reading stuff you probably were better off not reading, or whatever else you compromised or tweaked just because others have it or are doing it?

Q: Is this an issue you struggle with? Are you happy to hear when someone acquires something you've wanted for a very long time? Do you feel a lil' sting, and after you assimilate it, does it become easier to accept? Or more difficult? Or do you feel an immediate sense of happiness for her joy?

- What left an imprint in your heart?

Chapter 5
Embrace Your Own
Kind of Fabulous!

Q: Do you enjoy a loud atmosphere? Do you prefer quiet? Are you okay with both? Which one is better?

Q: Can you relate? Which person do you identify with? How does this make you feel? What can you learn from this? Let's discuss another situation.

Q: Can you relate? Which person do you identify with? How does this make you feel? What can you learn from this? Here is a different scenario.

Q: Can you relate? Which person do you identify with? How does this make you feel? What can you learn from this?

Q: Can you relate? Which person do you identify with? How does this make you feel? Is it easy to praise your friends' strengths, and can you be more patient in the area of weakness each of us possess?

- What left an imprint?

- What will you do for a friend this week?

Chapter 6
Fun, Sassy, Feisty,
or Sweet Chick

Q: Is this you? Do you embrace being a fun-guinni? Why or why not? Is there something you would like to change?

Q: What word or words describe you?

Q: What interesting things did you find out about yourself?

Q: What interesting things did you find out about your closest friend or friends?

Q: Is this you? Do you embrace being a sassy-choly? Why or why not? Is there something you would like to change?

Q: What word or words describe you?

What interesting things did you find out about yourself?

What interesting things did you find out about your closest friend or friends?

Q: Is this you? Do you embrace being go-leric? Why or why not? Is there something you would like to change?

Q: What word or words describe you?

Q: What interesting things did you find out about yourself?

Q: What interesting things did you find out about your closest friend or friends?

Q: Is this you? Do you embrace being a sweet-matic? Why or why not? Is there something you would like to change?

Q: What word or words describe you?

Q: What interesting things did you find out about yourself?

Q: What interesting things did you find out about your closest friend?

More questions—let's answer them together.

Q: Did you find out what your temperament is? Which is the predominant one? What others are you a mix of?

Q: Name a few important things you learned from this.

Q: How can you use your temperament or personality to bless other people?

Q: Is there an area of weakness you need to work on?

Q: What did you discover to be your strength?

Q: Did you find this helpful? What new things did you learn about your friends' strengths and weaknesses?

- What left an imprint?

Chapter 7
Triggers That Make You Say, "Hmm"

No test or temptation that comes your way is beyond the course of what others have had to face. All you need to remember is that God will never let you down; he'll never let you be pushed past your limit; he'll always be there to help you come through it. (1 Cor. 10:13)

Finally, brothers and sisters, whatever is true, whatever is noble, whatever is right, whatever is pure, whatever is lovely, whatever is admirable—if anything is excellent or praiseworthy—think about such things. (Phil. 4:8 NIV)

Q: How can this verse help you next time you catch yourself ignoring the yellow light trigger alerts?

Summing it all up, friends, I'd say you'll do best by filling your minds and meditating on things true, noble, reputable, authentic, compelling,

gracious—the best, not the worst; the beautiful, not the ugly; things to praise, not things to
curse. Put into practice what you learned from
me, what you heard and saw and realized. Do
that, and God, who makes everything work_
together, will work you into his most excellent
harmonies. (Phil. 4:8–9 MSG)

Q: How can you divert your thought process from twisted thinking
to thoughts worthy of praise?

Look what it says in Luke:

A good man brings good things out of the
good stored up in his heart, and an evil man
brings evil things out of the evil stored up in his
heart. For the mouth speaks what the heart is
full of. (Luke 6:45 NIV)

Q: Can you think of a time when this verse proved its point?

Q: What areas of sin are you particularly prone to? Is there a trigger in your life that causes you to sin? Why do you think it's important to be aware of your triggers?

Sin can be a powerful thing, but God is an almighty powerful sovereign God who can defeat anything. Never forget that!

> As long as you did what you felt like doing, ignoring God, you didn't have to bother with right thinking or right living, or right anything for that matter. But do you call that a free life? What did you get out of it? Nothing you're proud of now. Where did it get you? A dead end. But now that you've found you don't have to listen to sin tells you what to do, and have discovered the delight of listening to God telling you, what a surprise! A whole, healed, put-together life right now, with more and more of life on the way! Work hard for sin your whole life and your pension is death. But God's gift is real life, eternal life, delivered by Jesus, our Master. (Rom. 6:20–23)

Q: In what areas of your life have you felt as if sin has controlled you? Is there something that hinders you from taking the escape route? In what areas of your life have you felt like you've overcome sin through God's strength?

Q: Can you explain in your own words what this verse means? What do you think death means in this verse?

- What left an imprint in your heart?

- What will you do to control your triggers this week?

Chapter 8
Loved and Accepted As-Is

If you hold on to my teaching, you are really my disciples. Then you will know the truth, and the truth will set you free. (John 8:31–32)

Q: How many times have you acted like something you aren't only to fit in? How many times have you judged based on what others have told you about someone? What have you learned about judging without really knowing the truth? Can anyone share an incident with either of these scenarios?

I do not sit with the deceitful men, nor do I associate with hypocrites. (Ps. 26:4 NIV)

I do not sit with false persons, nor fellowship with pretenders. (Ps. 26:4 AMP)

Ouch! Thank God for His mercy and grace! Let's read what it says in Matthew about being a hypocrite.

Don't pick on people, jump on their failures, and criticize their faults—unless, of course, you want the same treatment. That critical spirit has a way of boomeranging. It's easy to see a smudge on your neighbor's face and be oblivious to the ugly sneer on your own. Do you have the nerve to say, 'Let me wash your face for you,' when your own face is distorted by contempt? It's this whole traveling road-show mentality all over again, playing a holier-than-thou part instead of just living your part. Wipe that ugly sneer off your own face, and you might be fit to offer a washcloth to your neighbor. (Matt. 7:1–5 MSG)

Q: What do you think about Matthew 7:1–5? Have you ever been in a situation where you were stuck seeing only the speck in your friend's, brother's, husband's, etc., eye but didn't see the timber in your eye?

Q: Have you ever met anyone who acts holier than thou so much that it's uncomfortable to share certain things because you feel you'll be looked upon as weird or worse? Does anyone have the courage to share?

To the Jews who had believed him, Jesus said,
"If you hold on to my teaching, you are really
my disciples. Then you will know the truth, and
the truth will set you free." (John 8:31–32 NIV)

Q: Do you remember an incident where you pretended or flat–out

lied about something or someone, and it was eating you up inside,

but when you told the truth about it, it was like a ton of weight

had been lifted? The truth sets you free.

Word became flesh and made his dwelling
among us. We have seen his glory, the glory
of the one and only Son, who came from the
Father, full of grace and truth. (John 1:14 NIV)

Q: Are there things you don't like about yourself that you are

committed to work on and improve? Are there certain things

about yourself that you once didn't like but you've learned to

appreciate? Name two.

Q: Do you know an Ellie? Are you an Ellie? When you think of finally being you, how far along in the process do you think you are on a scale of one to ten, with ten being the closest? What areas do you struggle with in becoming who you truly are?

Q: Have you experienced being open and transparent? What was the outcome? Are you in a place where you would rather wear a mask because it's more comfortable or safer? Do you know someone who is constantly hiding behind a mask? Which mask? How do you feel about this? Do you know someone who is totally genuine? How does being around her make you feel?

Q: What do you say about the following statement: "We attach a higher value on keeping the peace than speaking freely or standing up for someone"?

Q: Do you consider yourself to be someone who would rather stay quiet or speak out when someone is bashing your friend? Why do you find this to be or not to be important?

Q: Have you ever been with a group of people in which you weren't strong enough to abstain from participating in a conversation, maybe even agreeing to unkind comments about people you call friends; perhaps adding to or deducting from the truth; volunteering unsolicited information just to feel a sense of belonging or to make others believe you think like they do; or possibly even using false flattery? In other words, have you participated in gossip?

Q: Have you noticed you defend the other person by not refraining but actually stopping the conversation? Are you okay with being seen sometimes as a feisty chick? The one who tries to make sure others are reminded there are always two sides to every story... Or would you rather stay quiet and appear serene and well composed to keep the peace? Why or why not?

How awful, right? It is even more so when we pretend we've never been there.

Q: How do you stop this from happening?

Q: Have you ever been so annoyed or angry at a friend that whenever the chance comes up, you still vent about it?

Fight this war with the sword that cuts deep: the Word

> Without wood a fire goes out; without gossips, conflict calms down. (Prov. 26:20 CEB)

> Gossips reveal secrets; don't associate with those who talk too much. (Prov. 20:19 CEB)

> Destructive people produce conflict; gossips alienate close friends. (Prov. 16:28 CEB)

If we'd realize there is spiritual warfare going on all the time, we'd prepare and be stronger to fight against it. Unfortunately, we are unaware of it. Here is another sword to help you fight spiritual warfare:

Meditate on this:

> And that about wraps it up. God is strong, and he wants you strong. So take everything the Master has set out for you, well-made weapons of the best materials. And put them to use so you will be able to stand up to everything the Devil throws your way. This is no afternoon athletic contest that we'll walk away from and forget about in a couple of hours. This is for keeps, a life-or-death fight to the finish against the Devil and all his angels. Be prepared. You're up against far more than you can handle on your own. Take all the help you can get, every weapon God has issued, so that when it's all over but the shouting you'll still be on your feet. Truth, righteousness, peace, faith, and salvation are more than words. Learn how to apply them. You'll need them throughout your life. God's Word is an indispensable weapon. In the same way, prayer is essential in this ongoing warfare. Pray hard and long. Pray for your brothers and sisters. Keep your eyes open. Keep each other's spirits up so that no one falls behind or drops out. (Eph. 6:10–18 MSG)

Q: Any thoughts? Write about what resonates loudest.

Q: When was the last time you tried to justify a story or a point you made, or maybe even a supposed joke you told, but you knew deep inside it was a lie? What can you do differently?

Q: How many times do words slip when you hang out with friends who use this language? Are you strong enough to not let your friends' habits influence you? Maybe you fall into drinking more than you wanted, smoking, over-shopping, or so many other things. Have you stopped and taken the time to acknowledge the change in behavior when you are with certain people? Check yourself next time.

You, my darling, are awesome and are accepted as-is—only God loves you too much to leave you the same! His love transforms!

- What left an imprint in your heart?

- What will you do to control your triggers this week?

Chapter 9
Diversity Is a Beautiful Thing!

Q: Have you heard the voice inside that tells you to get involved and do something but you are afraid of taking on this challenge? What do you think hinders you from this calling?

Q: Is this you? Can you see clearer how something so simple can be a huge help? Will you make the effort to learn more and get more involved? Why?

Q: Have you been in this place before, knowing the truth but ignoring it?

Q: Have you ever met people you admire but they seem too good, like you could never reach their level? What about meeting people who seem pretty faithful and firm in their convictions but who struggle like you and me? What are your thoughts?

Q: Were you ever afraid of committing to become a true follower? Why? How did it change? How do you feel now? Or in all truthfulness, do you believe this lifestyle is boring and will limit you from many things? How?

Q: Have you ever been to a church where you found it more comfortable than another? What factored into your viewpoint? Have you ever been criticized for the church you attend? How do you handle it? Have you been criticized for your beliefs and convictions? How do you handle it? Have you criticized other people's beliefs and convictions?

Q: Have you ever attended a church that was so different from what you expected or were used to that it actually made a huge impact in a positive way? How? Have you ever attended a church that was so different from what you expected or were used to that it turned you off?

Check out diversity:

Q: What is your favorite store?

Q: Are you a sweets or salty type of gal?

Q: Do you prefer the beach or the pool?

Q: Dog or cat?

Q: Casual or fancy?

Q: Vanilla or chocolate?

Q: Skittles or Starbursts?

Q: Day or night?

Q: One or two friends or bigger groups?

Q: Law & Order or Modern Family?

Q: Hamburgers or tacos?

Q: PC (politically correct) or straight to the point?

Q: Winter, spring, summer, or fall?

Q: Comfort or suffer pain for beauty?

Q: Hershey's with almonds or plain?

Q: What new things have you learned from others who are the opposite of you? And what have you learned from those who are the same?

Q: Do you know the depth of God's love for you? Do you know that you have incredible potential to do great things? Do you realize it takes courage to go out of your comfort zone to take the first step?

Q: What will it take for you to begin a journey that serves others? How can you exalt your friends' strengths? How can you be a true cheerleader and help or promote your fellow giG sisters' endeavors and events or life-changing projects? What can you do to help make other people's dreams become a reality?

Finding diversity in everything is a beautiful thing!

> Let's not get tired of doing good, because in time we'll have a harvest if we don't give up. (Gal 6:9 CEB)

Make a wish ...

My wish is to recognize who
God created me to be and bring
smiles to those around me!

Who are you?

Thoughts:

What did you like the best about this study?

What was your favorite chapter? Why?

Did you become closer to someone while reading this guide?

What left an imprint in your heart about yourself? About those close to you?

Do you think you've made some real friends?

Did you witness miracles during your time spent with giG? Write them down to remind you of God's amazing grace.

Did you make a commitment to serve in your church or anywhere else? Did you find a soft spot for a certain cause? Which one?

Write why you would or would not recommend this guide to a girlfriend. Was there a negative experience that taught you a positive lesson?

List of resolutions:

If you are interested in joining an organization and help make a change in our world, start with one person a time!

Go to: www.sendmefoundation.com

And do not forget to do good and to share with others, for with such sacrifices God is pleased. (Heb. 13:16 NIV)

Diversity is a beautiful thing!

It's what makes the world go 'round ...

Embrace it!

Remember, you don't have to do everything, but do something!

Bibliography

Feinberg, Margaret. *Being Yourself, How Do I Take Off This Mask?* Nashville, TN: Thomas Nelson, 2008.

_____. *Friendship Cultivating the Relationships that Enrich Our Lives.* Nashville, TN: Thomas Nelson, 2009.

Hatmaker, Jen. *Girl Talk.* Colorado Springs, CO: NavPress, 2007.

Wagner, Holly. *Godchicks.* Nashville, TN: Thomas Nelson, 2003.